COMBATIVES

HEADQUARTERS
DEPARTMENT OF THE ARMY

DISTRIBUTION RESTRICTION: Approved for public release; distribution is unlimited.

By Order of the Secretary of the Army:

ERIC K. SHINSEKI
General, United States Army
Chief of Staff

Official:

JOEL B. HUDSON
Administrative Assistant to the
Secretary of the Army
0202404

DISTRIBUTION:

Active Army, Army National Guard, and U.S. Army Reserve: To be distributed in accordance with the initial distribution number 110176, requirements for FM 3-25.150.

FIELD MANUAL
No. 3-25.150

HEADQUARTERS
DEPARTMENT OF THE ARMY
WASHINGTON, DC, 18 January 2002

COMBATIVES

TABLE OF CONTENTS

		Page
PREFACE		iv

CHAPTER 1. INTRODUCTION
1-1.	Definition of Combatives	1-1
1-2.	Purposes of Combative Training	1-1
1-3.	Basic Principles	1-1
1-4.	Safety	1-2

CHAPTER 2. TRAINING
Section	I.	Train-the-Trainer	2-1
	2-1.	Responsibilities of Trainers	2-1
	2-2.	Safety Precautions	2-1
Section	II.	Unit Training	2-2
	2-3.	Basic or One-Station Unit Training	2-3
	2-4.	Unit Sustainment Training Program	2-4
Section	III.	Training Areas	2-4
	2-5.	Training Formations	2-4
	2-6.	Matted Room	2-5
	2-7.	Pit Construction	2-5
	2-8.	Bayonet Assault Course	2-6
Section	IV.	Teaching Techniques	2-12
	2-9.	Warm-Ups and Stretches	2-12
	2-10.	Crawl, Walk, and Run	2-18
	2-11.	Demonstrations	2-18
	2-12.	Execution by the Numbers	2-19
	2-13.	Execution at Combat Speed	2-19
	2-14.	Drills	2-19
	2-15.	Training Pads and Other Protective Equipment	2-19

DISTRIBUTION RESTRICTION: Approved for public release; distribution is unlimited.

*This publication supersedes FM 21-150, 30 September 1992.

Page

CHAPTER 3. BASIC GROUND-FIGHTING TECHNIQUES
Section   I. Dominant Body Position 3-1
                        3-1.   Back Mount 3-1
                        3-2.   Front Mount 3-2
                        3-3.   Guard 3-3
                        3-4.   Side Control 3-4
Section   II. Basic Techniques 3-4
                        3-5.   Body Positioning Moves 3-4
                        3-6.   Finishing Moves 3-24
                        3-7.   Drills 3-40
                        3-8.   Defense Against Headlocks 3-41

CHAPTER 4. ADVANCED GROUND-FIGHTING TECHNIQUES
Section   I. Advanced Attacks 4-1
                        4-1.   Advanced Body Positions 4-1
                        4-2.   Pass the Guard 4-2
                        4-3.   Attacks from the Mount 4-14
                        4-4.   Attacks from the Back Mount 4-25
                        4-5.   Attacks from the Guard 4-30
                        4-6.   Knee Mount 4-41
                        4-7.   Leg Attacks 4-52
Section   II. Strikes 4-57
                        4-8.   Pass the Guard 4-57
                        4-9.   Striking from Side Control 4-63
                        4-10.   Defending Against Strikes in the Guard 4-65

CHAPTER 5. TAKEDOWNS AND THROWS
                        5-1.   Breakfalls 5-1
                        5-2.   Closing the Distance and Achieving the Clinch 5-4
                        5-3.   Throw and Takedown Techniques 5-6
                        5-4.   Defending Against Headlocks 5-13
                        5-5.   Takedowns from Against a Wall 5-21
                        5-6.   Double Leg Attack 5-24
                        5-7.   Single Leg Attacks 5-28
                        5-8.   Attacks from the Rear 5-31

CHAPTER 6. STRIKES
                        6-1.   Arm Strikes 6-1
                        6-2.   Punching Combinations 6-6
                        6-3.   Kicks 6-6
                        6-4.   Transition Between Ranges 6-9

Page

CHAPTER 7. HANDHELD WEAPONS
Section   I. Offensive Techniques..7-1
                7-1.   Angles of Attack...7-1
                7-2.   Rifle with Fixed Bayonet 7-2
                7-3.   Bayonet/Knife 7-23
                7-4.   Knife-Against-Rifle Sequence 7-24
                7-5.   Advanced Weapons Techniques and Training......................7-28
Section   II. Field-Expedient Weapons 7-29
                7-6.   Entrenching Tool...7-29
                7-7.   Three-Foot Stick..7-33
                7-8.   Six-Foot Pole...7-36

CHAPTER 8. STANDING DEFENSE
Section   I. Unarmed Opponent 8-1
                8-1.   Defense Against Chokes 8-1
                8-2.   Defense Against Bear Hugs 8-7
Section   II. Armed Opponent 8-13
                8-3.   Defense Against Armed Opponent 8-13
                8-4.   Defense Against a Knife 8-14
                8-5.   Unarmed Defense Against a Rifle with Fixed Bayonet..........8-22

CHAPTER 9. GROUP TACTICS
Section   I. Lethal Force Scenarios 9-1
                9-1.   Range...9-1
                9-2.   Control...9-1
                9-3.   Finishing..9-1
Section   II. Restrictive Force Scenarios......................................9-2
                9-4.   Two Against One 9-2
                9-5.   Three Against Two...9-2
                9-6.   Parity..9-2
                9-7.   One Against Two 9-2
                9-8.   Two Against Three..9-3

APPENDIX A. SITUATIONAL TRAINING A-1
APPENDIX B. COMPETITIONS B-1
GLOSSARY Glossary-1
REFERENCES References-1
INDEX Index-1

PREFACE

This field manual contains information and guidance pertaining to rifle-bayonet fighting and hand-to-hand combat. The hand-to-hand combat portion of this manual is divided into basic and advanced training. This manual serves as a guide for instructors, trainers, and soldiers in the art of instinctive rifle-bayonet fighting.

The proponent for this publication is the United States Army Infantry School. Send comments and recommendations on DA Form 2028 (Recommended Changes to Publications and Blank Forms) directly to Commandant, United States Army Infantry School, ATTN: ATSH-RB, Fort Benning, GA, 31905-5430.

Unless this publication states otherwise, masculine nouns and pronouns do not refer exclusively to men.

CHAPTER 1
INTRODUCTION

Very few people have ever been killed with the bayonet or saber, but the fear of having their guts explored with cold steel in the hands of battle-maddened men has won many a fight.

-PATTON

1-1. DEFINITION OF COMBATIVES

Hand-to-hand combat is an engagement between two or more persons in an empty-handed struggle or with hand-held weapons such as knives, sticks, or projectile weapons that cannot be fired. Proficiency in hand-to-hand combat is one of the fundamental building blocks for training the modern soldier.

1-2. PURPOSES OF COMBATIVES TRAINING

Soldiers must be prepared to use different levels of force in an environment where conflict may change from low intensity to high intensity over a matter of hours. Many military operations, such as peacekeeping missions or noncombatant evacuation, may restrict the use of deadly weapons. Hand-to-hand combatives training will save lives when an unexpected confrontation occurs.

More importantly, combatives training helps to instill courage and self-confidence. With competence comes the understanding of controlled aggression and the ability to remain focused while under duress. Training in combatives includes hard and arduous physical training that is, at the same time, mentally demanding and carries over to other military pursuits. The overall effect of combatives training is—

- The culmination of a successful physical fitness program, enhancing individual and unit strength, flexibility, balance, and cardiorespiratory fitness.
- Building personal courage, self confidence, self-discipline, and esprit de corps.

1-3. BASIC PRINCIPLES

Underlying all combatives techniques are principles the hand-to-hand fighter must apply to successfully defeat an opponent. The natural progression of techniques, as presented in this manual, will instill these principles into the soldier.

a. **Mental Calm.** During a fight a soldier must keep his ability to think. He must not allow fear or anger to control his actions.

b. **Situational Awareness.** Things are often going on around the fighters that could have a direct impact on the outcome of the fight such as opportunity weapons or other personnel joining the fight.

c. **Suppleness.** A soldier cannot always count on being bigger and stronger than the enemy. He should, therefore, never try to oppose the enemy in a direct test of strength. Supple misdirection of the enemy's strength allows superior technique and fight strategy to overcome superior strength.

d. **Base.** Base refers to the posture that allows a soldier to gain leverage from the ground. Generally, a soldier must keep his center of gravity low and his base wide—much like a pyramid.

e. **Dominant Body Position**. Position refers to the location of the fighter's body in relation to his opponent's. A vital principle when fighting is to gain control of the enemy by controlling this relationship. Before any killing or disabling technique can be applied, the soldier must first gain and maintain one of the dominant body positions (Chapter 3, Section I).

f. **Distance**. Each technique has a window of effectiveness based upon the amount of space between the two combatants. The fighter must control the distance between himself and the enemy in order to control the fight.

g. **Physical Balance.** Balance refers to the ability to maintain equilibrium and to remain in a stable upright position.

h. **Leverage.** A fighter uses the parts of his body to create a natural mechanical advantage over the parts of the enemy's body. By using leverage, a fighter can have a greater effect on a much larger enemy.

1-4. SAFETY

The Army's combatives program has been specifically designed to train the most competent fighters in the shortest possible time in the safest possible manner.

a. **General Safety Precautions.** The techniques of Army combatives should be taught in the order presented in this manual. They are arranged to not only give the natural progression of techniques, but to present the more dangerous techniques after the soldiers have established a familiarity with the dynamics of combative techniques in general. This will result in fewer serious injuries from the more dynamic moves.

b. **Supervision.** The most important safety consideration is proper supervision. Because of the potentially dangerous nature of the techniques involved, combatives training must always be conducted under the supervision of qualified leaders.

c. **Training Areas.** Most training should be conducted in an area with soft footing such as a grassy or sandy area. If training mats are available, they should be used. A hard surface area is not appropriate for combatives training.

d. **Chokes.** Chokes are the best way to end a fight. They are the most effective way to incapacitate an enemy and, with supervision, are also safe enough to apply in training exactly as on the battlefield.

e. **Joint Locks.** In order to incapacitate an enemy, attacks should be directed against large joints such as the elbow, shoulder, or knee. Attacks on most of these joints are very painful long before causing any injury, which allows full-force training to be conducted without significant risk of injury. The exceptions are wrist attacks and twisting knee attacks. The wrist is very easily damaged, and twisting the knee does not become painful until it is too late. Therefore, these attacks should be taught with great care and should not be allowed in sparring or competitions.

f. **Striking.** Striking is an inefficient way to incapacitate an enemy. Strikes are, however, an important part of an overall fight strategy and can be very effective in manipulating the opponent into unfavorable positions. Striking can be practiced with various types of protective padding such as boxing gloves. Defense can be practiced using reduced force blows. Training should be continuously focused on the realities of fighting.

CHAPTER 2
TRAINING

This chapter discusses the trainer's role in teaching and sustaining effective hand-to-hand combat. It also discusses unit training, training areas, teaching techniques, and safety precautions that must be considered before conducting combatives training.

Section I. TRAIN-THE-TRAINER

Professional instruction is the key to success in combatives training. Instructors must be physically fit and highly proficient in the demonstration and practical application of the skills. They must review and be familiar with this manual. Confidence, enthusiasm, and technical expertise are essential for success in teaching hand-to-hand combat. Assistant instructors must also be properly trained to help supervise and demonstrate maneuvers. Selecting the trainers is the first step in establishing an effective program.

2-1. RESPONSIBILITIES OF TRAINERS

Diligent effort is needed to perfect the various hand-to-hand combat techniques, to apply them instinctively, and to teach others to safely master them. The following instructor responsibilities are the core of planning and executing combatives training.

a. Seek maximum efficiency with minimum effort. Continually strive to reduce all unnecessary explanations, movement, and activity. Streamline the training without compromising content, efficiency, or safety.

b. Stress cooperation and technical mastery. Promote suppleness and controlling aggression.

c. Reinforce the details of each technique and provide positive feedback when warranted. Use occasional humor to motivate soldiers, but avoid degrading or insulting them.

d. Ensure serviceable training aids are present in sufficient quantities for all soldiers being trained. Ensure training areas are well maintained and free of dangerous obstructions.

e. Ensure instructors and assistant instructors are well-rehearsed and prepared before all training sessions. Conduct instructor training at least five hours weekly to maintain a high skill level.

f. Develop as many skilled combatives instructors for each unit as possible. Instructor-to-soldier ratios should not exceed 1 instructor for 20 soldiers. Encourage after-duty training and education for instructors.

g. Require strict discipline of all soldiers.

2-2. SAFETY PRECAUTIONS

To prevent injuries, the instructor must consider the following safety precautions before conducting combatives training.

a. Supervise all practical work closely and constantly. Never leave a group unsupervised.

b. Familiarize the soldiers with each maneuver by a complete explanation and demonstration before they attempt the moves.

c. Do not allow the soldiers to get ahead of the instruction.

d. Ensure the training partner offers no resistance, but allows the maneuver to be freely executed during the learning stages and while perfecting the techniques.

e. Ensure there is adequate space between soldiers during all practical work—for example, allow at least an 8-foot square for each pair of soldiers.

f. Ensure that soldiers empty their pockets, and remove their jewelry, and identification tags before training.

g. Stress that only simulated strikes to vital points, such as the head, neck, and groin area are to be executed. Soldiers may use light blows to other vulnerable areas; however, they must exercise caution at all times.

h. Ensure that soldiers understand the use of both physical tapping and verbal signals to indicate to the partner when to stop the pressure in grappling and choking techniques.

i. Make sure soldiers warm up and stretch properly before practical work.

j. Teach and practice falls before conducting throws.

k. Ensure that the soldier to be disarmed does not place his finger in the trigger guard during rifle and bayonet disarming.

l. Make sure soldiers keep scabbards on knives and bayonets firmly attached to rifles while learning bayonet disarming methods.

m. Use bayonet scabbards or rubber knives during knife disarming training.

n. If utilizing a sawdust pit, inspect all sandbags on retaining wall before conduct of training to ensure that all bags are serviceable, at least 75 percent full, and that the entire retaining wall is covered with sandbags. Any bag placed where personnel are likely to fall will be filled with the same consistency filler as the sawdust in the pit and will also provide a minimum of 6 inches of sawdust.

o. Maintain a buffer zone of 6 feet from retainer wall and demonstration area during all training, especially training requiring throws and takedowns by students.

p. Rake the training pit to loosen sawdust and remove all sharp objects. Properly inspect the pit so that all safety hazards are removed before instruction or demonstrations are executed.

q. Perform inspections of the depth of sawdust with enough time before training to resurface the pit. Remember that new sawdust will need to be raked and inspected for foreign objects that may cause injuries.

Section II. UNIT TRAINING

Entry-level soldiers receive a training base in combatives during basic training and one-station unit training (OSUT). Advanced individual training (AIT) commanders should review the training presented during basic training and, as time permits, expand into the more advanced techniques discussed in this manual. For soldiers to achieve and sustain proficiency levels regular units must incorporate combatives into an organized training program to include situational training exercises (Appendix A).

2-3. BASIC OR ONE-STATION UNIT TRAINING

This is a suggested training program for basic training or OSUT. It is based on ten hours of available training time, divided into five periods of two hours each. Training should start with ground grappling, which is not only easier both to teach and to learn, but also provides a sound base for the more difficult standing techniques. A program should not begin with techniques that will take a long time to master. The result would be almost uniform disillusionment with combatives in general.

a. **Period 1 (2 hours).**
- Introduction to combatives safety.
- Combat demonstration performed by instructors or trainers to gain attention and to motivate soldiers.
- Warm-ups and stretches.
- Stand up in base.
- Escape the mount by trap and roll.
- Pass the guard.
- Achieve the mount.
- Drill No. 1, 10 to 15 repetitions; escape the mount, pass the guard, achieve the mount, in sequence.
- Escape the mount by shrimp to the guard.
- Escape the mount drill.

b. **Period 2 (2 hours).**
- Warm-ups and stretches.
- Drill No. 1, ten repetitions.
- Arm push and roll to the rear mount.
- Escape the rear mount.
- Drill No. 2: Arm push and roll to the back mount, escape the back mount.
- Grappling for position, five minutes and then change partners. Repeat for duration of class.

c. **Period 3 (2 hours).**
- Warm-ups and stretches.
- Drill No. 1, ten repetitions.
- Drill No. 2, ten repetitions.
- Introduction to choking.
- Rear naked choke.
- Cross collar choke from the mount and guard.
- Front guillotine choke.

d. **Period 4 (2 hours).**
- Warm-ups and stretches.
- Drill No. 1, ten repetitions.
- Drill No. 2, ten repetitions.
- Bent arm bar from the mount and cross mount.
- Straight arm bar from the mount.
- Straight arm bar from the guard.
- Sweep from straight arm bar attempt.

e. **Period 5 (2 hours).**
- Warm-ups and stretches.
- Drill No. 1, ten repetitions.
- Drill No. 2, ten repetitions.
- Review.
- Rules introduction.
- Competition.

2-4. UNIT SUSTAINMENT TRAINING PROGRAM

Command emphasis is the key to a successful combatives program. Combatives training sessions should be regular, and should be included on unit training schedules at company and platoon level.

a. Successful unit combatives programs continue to focus on the core techniques taught in the basic training or OSUT program. Mastery of these moves will result in more proficient fighters than exposure to a large number of techniques will.

b. As the level of proficiency rises the natural progression of moves is as follows:
- Advanced ground grappling.
- Takedowns.
- Strikes and kicks.
- Fight strategy.
- Situational training.

c. Primary trainers should be designated at all levels. Regular training sessions with these trainers will ensure the quality of training at the small unit level.

d. Primary trainers should be of the appropriate rank; for instance, a platoon primary trainer should be a squad leader or the platoon sergeant to ensure that the training actually occurs.

e. Modern combatives allow soldiers to compete safely. To inspire the pursuit of excellence, individual soldiers may compete during organizational day. Leaders may also call squads, sections, or individuals to compete randomly as a method of inspecting training levels. All combatives competitions should be conducted IAW rules established in Appendix B of this manual. However, competition should not become the focus of combatives training, but remain a tool to inspire further training.

Section III. TRAINING AREAS

An advantage of combatives training is that it can be conducted almost anywhere with little preparation of the training area.

2-5. TRAINING FORMATIONS

Formations used for physical training may also be used for combatives training (FM 21-20). If the extended rectangular formation is used, the first and third ranks should face the second and fourth ranks so that each soldier is directly across him a partner.

A large, grassy, outdoor area free of obstructions is suitable for training. Each pair of soldiers should have an 8-foot square training space. When practicing throws or disarming techniques, soldiers need twice the normal interval between ranks. Instructors also pair soldiers according to height and weight.

2-6. MATTED ROOM

Because inclement weather can be a training distracter, the best training area is an indoor, climate-controlled facility with both padded floor and walls. Mats should be sufficiently firm to allow free movement, but provide enough impact absorption to allow safe throws and takedowns.

2-7. PIT CONSTRUCTION

A common area for teaching hand-to-hand combat is a sawdust pit. Sawdust pits are designed to teach throws and falls safely, but are not very suitable for ground fighting. Figure 2-1 shows a training area for 200 soldiers with a sawdust pit surrounding an instructor and a demonstrator platform.

a. To construct the pit, dig out and level an area 50 meters wide, and build a retaining wall at least 24 inches high. The wall can be cinderblocks, sandbags, or dirt if other materials are not available. (To prevent injuries when using a cinderblock retaining wall, cover the wall and the top of the wall with sandbags.) Place a layer of plastic sheeting on the ground to prevent the growth of grass and weeds, and place a sand base up to 12 inches deep on top of the plastic. Then, place a layer of sawdust about 6 inches deep on top of the sand.

b. Build a 14-foot square demonstration area (Figure 2-1) in the center of the pit with the same type of retaining wall described in paragraph a. This area should be large enough for two demonstrators and the primary instructor.

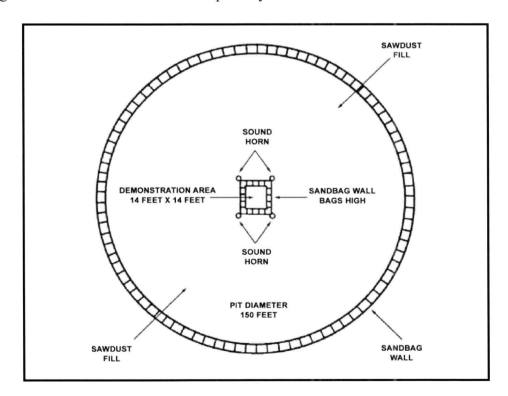

Figure 2-1. Combatives training pit.

2-8. BAYONET ASSAULT COURSE

The bayonet assault course provides the commander a unique training opportunity by allowing soldiers to employ rifle-bayonet fighting skills under simulated combat conditions. The course can be built and negotiated so that demands placed on the soldiers' abilities and on their endurance approach those experienced under combat conditions. Realistic sights and sounds of battle—fire, smoke, confusion, and pyrotechnics—can also be created to enhance realism. The training objectives of the bayonet assault course include:

- Improving rifle-bayonet fighting skills.
- Improving physical fitness and aggressiveness.
- Improving speed, strength, coordination, and accuracy.
- Providing realistic rifle-bayonet fighting under near combat conditions.
- Challenging the soldiers' determination and stamina, which are needed in combat.
- Providing an opportunity for team and squad leaders to develop their leadership and control measures.

a. **Safety.** The safety of the soldiers should be the primary concern of the instructor and his assistants. The best safety aids are constant control and supervision. In addition, instructors should brief soldiers at the beginning of each class on the requirements for safety during rifle-bayonet training. Instructors use the following safety measures:

(1) Bayonets must be fixed and unfixed only on command.

(2) Rifles should be grounded near the targets when the soldiers are ordered to move to the instructor's platform for explanations or demonstrations.

(3) A level surface that does not become slippery when wet should be provided for the training area.

(4) Left-handed soldiers should be positioned so they are opposite another left-handed soldier when working against the targets. This type of arrangement prevents possible injury when executing a series of movements.

(5) When using the M16 rifle against a target, the force of contact during the thrust movement may drive the hand gripping the small of the stock into the forward assist assembly (on the right-hand side of the weapon near the stock). To prevent injury to the hand, the soldier must maintain a firm grip on the small of the stock. Gloves should be worn as part of the training uniform when weather dictates.

b. **Layout.** The 300-meter-long course consists of a series of targets to attack, and obstacles to negotiate. Lay it out over natural terrain, preferably rough and wooded areas. Include natural obstacles such as streams, ravines, ridges, and thick vegetation. Build artificial obstacles such as entanglements, fences, log walls, hurdles, and horizontal ladders (Figure 2-2).

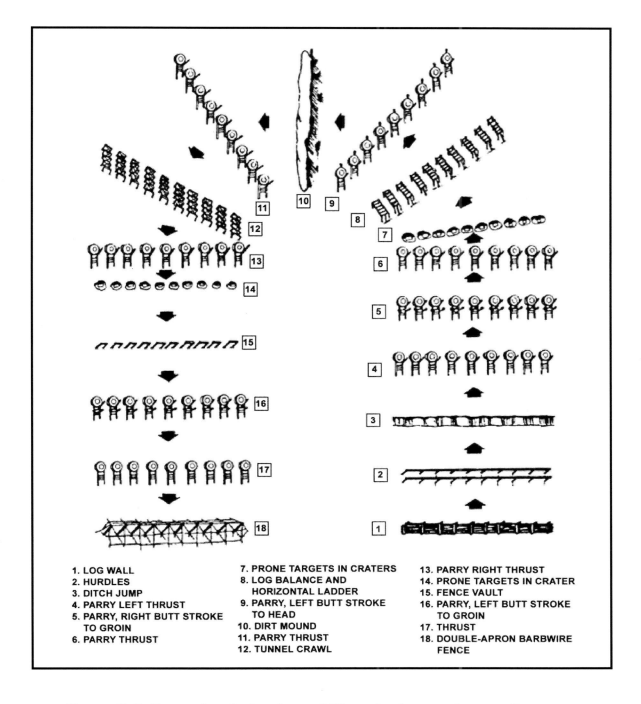

Figure 2-2. Example of nine-lane, 300-meter bayonet assault course.

1. LOG WALL
2. HURDLES
3. DITCH JUMP
4. PARRY LEFT THRUST
5. PARRY, RIGHT BUTT STROKE TO GROIN
6. PARRY THRUST
7. PRONE TARGETS IN CRATERS
8. LOG BALANCE AND HORIZONTAL LADDER
9. PARRY, LEFT BUTT STROKE TO HEAD
10. DIRT MOUND
11. PARRY THRUST
12. TUNNEL CRAWL
13. PARRY RIGHT THRUST
14. PRONE TARGETS IN CRATER
15. FENCE VAULT
16. PARRY, LEFT BUTT STROKE TO GROIN
17. THRUST
18. DOUBLE-APRON BARBWIRE FENCE

c. **Targets.** Use a variety of targets to provide experience in different attacks. The local Training and Support Center (TSC) can build the targets. Targets composed of old tires are appropriate as well as the Ivan-type targets used by range control—that is, the E-type silhouette, three-dimensional personnel target (large), FSN 6920-01-164-9625 or the F-type silhouette, three-dimensional personnel target (small), FSN 6920-00-T33-8777.

Targets should be durable but should not damage weapons. Place a sign near each target to indicate the type of attack to be used.

 d. **Usage**. An example of how to conduct the bayonet assault course is as follows:

 (1) *Task*. Negotiate the bayonet assault course.

 (2) *Conditions.* Given nine lanes on a 300-meter bayonet assault course over irregular terrain with four types of targets: thrust; parry thrust target; parry, butt stroke to the groin target; and parry, butt stroke to head target (Figure 2-3). The targets are marked with a sign to indicate the required attack. Given seven types of obstacles as shown in Figures 2-4 through 2-10. Given a soldier in battle dress uniform with load-carrying equipment and a rifle with a fixed bayonet.

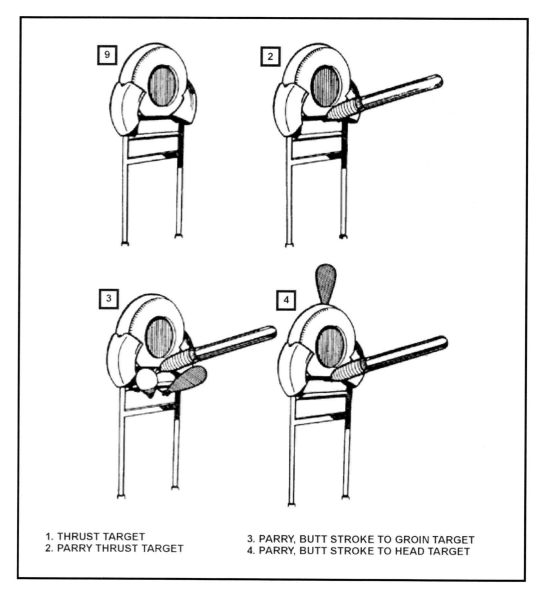

Figure 2-3. Types of targets.

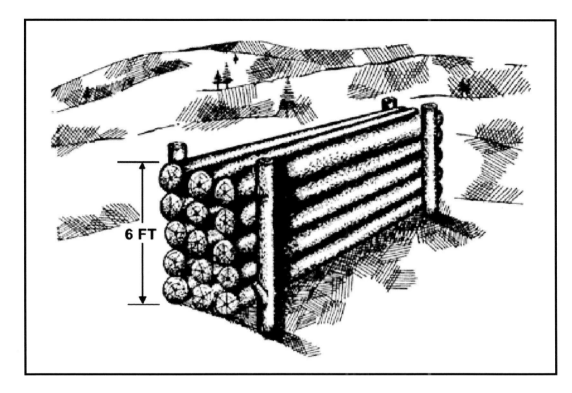

Figure 2-4. Log wall.

VARIABLE HEIGHTS - 27 INCHES MAXIMUM
VARIABLE INTERVALS

Figure 2-5. Hurdles.

Figure 2-6. Ditch jump.

Figure 2-7. Log balance and horizontal ladder.

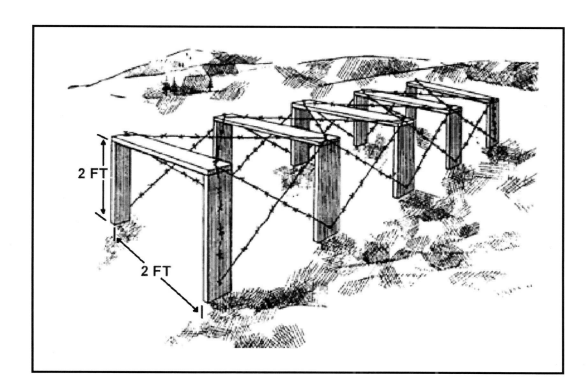

Figure 2-8. Tunnel crawl.

Figure 2-9. Fence vault.

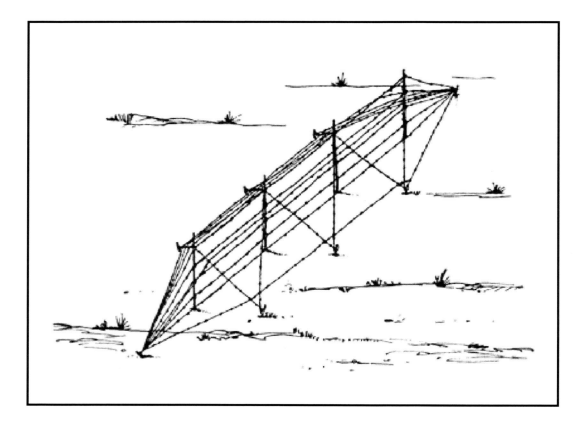

Figure 2-10. Double-apron barbwire fence.

(3) *Standards*. The course must be successfully negotiated by all soldiers in the class with each soldier obtaining kills on 75 percent of the total targets in his lane. The course must be negotiated in 5 minutes or less (about 30 seconds for each 50 meters and time to attack and negotiate obstacles).

```
                        WARNING
   To avoid injury, instructors ensure that the proper
   interval is constantly maintained.
```

Section IV. TEACHING TECHNIQUES

This section discusses a variety of effective teaching techniques to use while conducting combatives training.

2-9. WARM-UPS AND STRETCHES

Before combatives training, the soldier must be prepared for the upcoming physical stress. A warm-up period gradually increases the internal temperature of the body and the heart rate. Stretching prepares the ligaments, tendons, muscles, and heart for a workout, decreasing the chances of injury. After the initial warm-up, training drills can be used to further warm up. This allows for the maximum use of training time combining a portion of the warm up with building muscle memory, and refining the basic techniques.

a. **Warm-up Exercises**. To begin warm-up exercises, rotate the major joints—neck, shoulders, hips, and knees. The warm-up should include at least 7 to 10 minutes of stretching, running in place or jogging around the training area, and calisthenics. Grass drills and guerrilla exercises are good to use as a warm-up for combatives training. They condition the body through motion in all ranges, accustom the soldiers to contact with the ground, and promote aggressiveness.

b. **Stretching Exercises**. Any of the stretching exercises in FM 21-20 are recommended for hand-to-hand combat training. Five other exercises that increase flexibility in areas of the body that benefit hand-to-hand combat movements are as follows:

(1) *Backroll Stretch*.

(a) *Position*. Lay on ground on back with legs extended and arms by sides, palms down.

(b) *Action*. Raise legs over head and roll back as far as possible, trying to place toes on the ground behind head. Keep knees locked and feet and knees together; hold for 20 seconds (Figure 2-11). Gradually return to starting position. Repeat two or three times.

Figure 2-11. Backroll stretch.

(2) **Buddy-Assisted Splits (Leg Spreader).**

(a) *Position.* Sit on ground facing buddy with legs extended and spread as far as possible. Position feet inside ankles of buddy.

(b) *Action.* Interlock hands with buddy and alternate pulling one toward the other, causing the buddy to bend forward over the hips until a stretch is felt (Figure 2-12). Hold this position for 20 seconds, then alternate and have him pull you into a stretch. Do sequence two or three times.

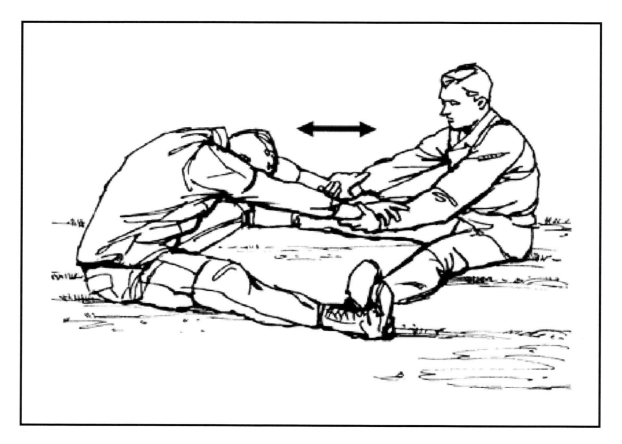

Figure 2-12. Buddy-assisted splits (leg spreader).

(3) *Buddy-Assisted Hamstring Stretch*.

(a) *Position*. Sit on ground with right leg extended to front and foot pointing up. Bend left leg with sole touching to inside of the right thigh. Have buddy kneel behind you with his hands on your shoulders (Figure 2-13).

(b) *Action*. Slowly bend forward from hips over the right leg and reach your hands toward ankles until stretch is felt (Figure 2-13). Hold this for 10 to 15 seconds. The buddy then applies downward pressure and allows you to adjust your stretch. Hold for 10 to 15 seconds and repeat. Alternate legs and positions after two or three sequences.

Figure 2-13. Buddy-assisted hamstring stretch.

(4) *Buddy-Assisted Groin (Butterfly) Stretch.*

(a) *Position.* Sit on ground with the soles of your feet together, close to the torso. Hold ankles with hands. Have buddy kneel behind you with his hands on your knees.

(b) *Action.* The buddy places his hands on top of your thighs at the knees. The buddy's weight is supported by your shoulders while little weight is placed on the thighs. Then, the buddy increases downward pressure on your thighs until stretch is felt (Figure 2-14). Hold for 20 seconds, then alternate positions.

Figure 2-14. Buddy-assisted groin (butterfly) stretch.

(5) **Buddy-Assisted Back Stretch.**

(a) *Position.* Stand back-to-back with buddy and interlock arms at your sides.

(b) *Action.* Bend forward at the waist and pull buddy up on your back over your hips. The buddy allows his back to arch and tells you when an adequate stretch is felt (Figure 2-15). Hold this position for 20 seconds, then, change places.

Figure 2-15. Buddy-assisted back stretch.

2-10. CRAWL, WALK, AND RUN

Training can be conducted using the crawl, walk, and run techniques, which may be applied on two levels.

a. **First Level**. The instructors use these techniques during each initial training session.

(1) *Crawl Phase*. New techniques are introduced, taught, demonstrated, and executed by the numbers.

(2) *Walk Phase*. During this phase, soldiers practice the new techniques by the numbers, but with more fluid movement and less instructor guidance.

(3) *Run Phase*. Soldiers execute the techniques at combat speed with supervision.

b. **Second Level**. The instructors use these techniques when developing unit combatives programs. Before conducting combatives training, the instructor considers the abilities and experience level of the soldiers to be trained. During training, those soldiers with prior martial arts experience can be a great asset; they may be used as demonstrators or as assistant instructors. The crawl, walk, run approach to unit training ensures a high skill level throughout the unit and minimizes the risk of training injuries.

(1) *Crawl Phase*. During the crawl phase, the instructor introduces combatives to the unit. Here, the basic skills that set the standards for advancement to other levels are mastered. Emphasis is placed on the basic ground fighting techniques, gradually introducing standup fighting and fight strategy. Studying the new techniques in this method ensures that the movements are correctly programmed into the soldiers' subconscious after a few repetitions.

(2) *Walk Phase*. Once a unit has developed a sufficient proficiency level in basic skills, begin the walk phase. Instructors introduce soldiers to more advanced ground fighting techniques and begin serious training on closing with the enemy and takedowns. Soldiers engage in full sparring and competitive matches.

(3) *Run Phase*. In the run phase, soldiers spar using slaps to represent striking during ground fighting, takedowns are practiced against an opponent with boxing gloves, and scenario driven training such as multiple opponent or restrictive equipment is used.

2-11. DEMONSTRATIONS

A well-coordinated demonstration and professional demonstrators are crucial for successful learning by soldiers. Unrehearsed presentations or inadequately trained demonstrators can immediately destroy the credibility of the training. Two methods are appropriate for demonstrating combative techniques based on the size of the group to be taught.

a. **Company-Size Formation or Larger**. The instructor or demonstrator uses the talk-through method. The primary instructor talks the demonstrators through the techniques by the numbers, and then the demonstrators execute at combat speed. The soldiers can see how to apply the move being taught in relation to the instructor or demonstrator. The primary instructor is free to control the rate of the demonstration and to stress key teaching points. The demonstrators must be skilled in properly applying the techniques so soldiers can adequately grasp the intended concepts.

b. **Platoon-Size Formation or Smaller.** A good method for demonstrating to a smaller formation is for the primary instructor to apply the technique being taught to an assistant instructor. The primary instructor talks himself through the demonstration. He stresses correct body movement and key teaching points as he does them.

2-12. EXECUTION BY THE NUMBERS

Instructors use execution by the numbers to break techniques down into step-by-step phases so soldiers can clearly see how the movements are developed from start to finish. Execution by the numbers also provides soldiers a way to see the mechanics of each technique. This teaching method allows the instructor to explain in detail the sequence of each movement. For example, on the command PHASE ONE, MOVE, the attacker throws a right-hand punch to the defender's face. At the same time, the defender steps to the inside of the attacker off the line of attack and moves into position for the right-hip throw. Assistant instructors are able to move freely throughout the training formation and make on-the-spot corrections.

2-13. EXECUTION AT COMBAT SPEED

When the instructor is confident that the soldiers being trained are skilled at executing a technique by the numbers, he has them execute it at combat speed. Executing movements at combat speed enables soldiers to see how effective a technique is. This builds the soldier's confidence in the technique, allows him to develop a clear mental picture of the principles behind the technique, and gives him confidence in his ability to perform the technique during an actual attack. For example, the command is, PASS THE GUARD AT COMBAT SPEED, MOVE. The soldiers then execute this technique from start to finish. It is important to remember that combat speed does not always mean very quickly. Speed requires space and space often favors the defender.

2-14. DRILLS

Drills are used to warm up, to reinforce the importance of dominant body position, and to perfect soldiers' basic skills through repetition. During these drills, basic positional techniques are repeated at the beginning of each training session with a different detail emphasized each session. In this way the emphasis is kept on perfecting the basic techniques, while at the same time making the best use of limited training time.

2-15. TRAINING PADS AND OTHER PROTECTIVE EQUIPMENT

Training pads are highly recommended to enhance training (Figure 2-16, page 2-20). They allow full-forced strikes by soldiers and protect their training partners. Although striking is a inefficient way to end a fight, it is a very important part of a fight. Pads enable soldiers to feel the effectiveness of striking techniques and to develop power in their striking. Instructors should encourage spirited aggressiveness. Pads can be tackle dummy pads or martial arts striking pads. Training pads can be requisitioned through supply channels or purchased locally.

a. The use of pads is especially recommended for knee-strike practice drills, and kicking drills. Ideally, the pad is placed on the outside of the training partner's thigh, protecting the common perennial nerve. Pads can also be held against the forearms in front of the head and face to allow practice of knee or elbow strikes to this area.

b. Other protective equipment, such as shin guards, can also be useful to practice with improvised weapons.

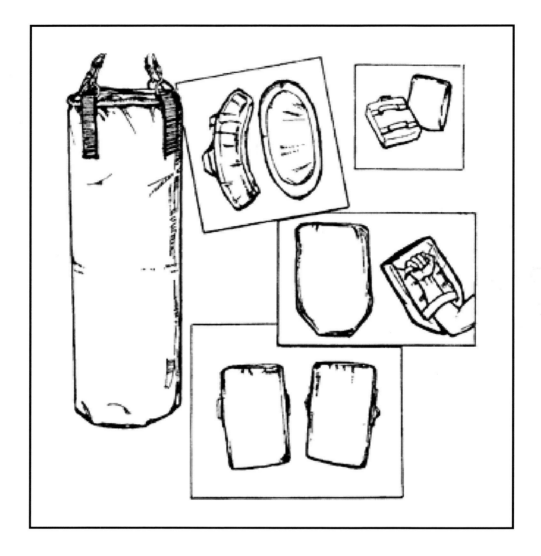

Figure 2-16. Training pads.

CHAPTER 3
BASIC GROUND-FIGHTING TECHNIQUES

Basic ground-fighting techniques build a fundamental understanding of dominant body position, which should be the focus of most combatives training before moving on to the more difficult standing techniques. Ground fighting is also where technique can most easily be used to overcome size and strength.

Section I. DOMINANT BODY POSITION

Before any killing or disabling technique can be applied, the soldier must first gain and maintain dominant body position. The leverage gained from dominant body position allows the fighter to defeat a stronger opponent. An appreciation for dominant position is fundamental to becoming a proficient fighter because it ties together what would otherwise be a long confusing list of unrelated techniques. If a finishing technique is attempted from dominant position and fails, the fighter can simply try again. If, on the other hand, a finishing technique is attempted from other than dominant position and fails, it will usually mean defeat. The dominant body positions will be introduced in order of precedence.

3-1. BACK MOUNT

The back mount gives the fighter the best control of the fight (Figure 3-1, page 3-2). From this position it is very difficult for the enemy to either defend himself or counterattack. Both legs should be wrapped around the enemy with the heels "hooked" inside his legs. One arm is under an armpit and the other is around the neck and the hands are clasped. Even though a fighter may find himself with his own back on the ground this is still the back mount.

CAUTION

While in the back mount, the fighter's feet should never be crossed because this would provide the enemy an opportunity for an ankle break.

Figure 3-1. Back mount.

3-2. FRONT MOUNT

The front mount (Figure 3-2) is dominant because it allows the fighter to strike the enemy with punches without the danger of effective return punches, and also provides the leverage to attack the enemy's upper body with joint attacks. Knees are as high as possible toward the enemy's armpits. This position should be held loosely to allow the enemy to turn over if he should try.

Figure 3-2. Front mount.

3-3. GUARD

If the fighter must be on the bottom, the guard position (Figure 3-3) allows the best defense and the only chance of offense. It is important initially for the fighter to lock his feet together behind the enemy's back to prevent him from simply pushing the fighter's knees down and stepping over them.

Figure 3-3. Guard.

3-4. SIDE CONTROL

Although side control (Figure 3-4) is not a dominant position, many times a fighter will find himself in this position, and he must be able to counter the enemy's defensive techniques. The fighter should place his elbow on the ground in the notch created by the enemy's head and shoulder. His other hand should be palm down on the ground on the near side of the enemy. The leg closest to the enemy's head should be straight and the other one bent so that the knee is near the enemy's hip. He should keep his head down to avoid knee strikes.

Figure 3-4. Side control.

Section II. BASIC TECHNIQUES

These basic techniques not only teach a fighter to understand dominant body position, but also provide an introduction to a systematic way of fighting on the ground. Almost all types of finishing moves are represented by the simplest and, at the same time, most effective example of the type. Before any time is spent on the more complex and harder to learn techniques presented later in this manual, the fighter must master these basics.

3-5. BODY POSITIONING MOVES

The key to developing good ground fighters is ingraining a feel for the dominant body positions and how they relate to each other.

a. **Stand up in Base.** This is the most basic technique. It allows the fighter to stand up in the presence of an enemy or potential enemy without compromising his base and thus making himself vulnerable to attack. The principles of body movement inherent in this technique make it so important that leaders should reinforce it every time a fighter stands up

(1) *Step 1* (Figure 3-5). The fighter assumes a seated posture resting on his strong side hand with his weak side arm resting comfortably on his bent knee. His feet should not be crossed.

Figure 3-5 Stand up in base, step 1.

(2) **Step 2** (Figure 3-6). Placing his weight on his strong side hand and weak side foot, the fighter picks up the rest of his body and swings his leg between his two posts, placing his foot behind his strong side hand. It is important that the knee should be behind the same side arm as shown.

Figure 3-6. Stand up in base, step 2.

(3) **Step 3** (Figure 3-7). After placing his weight on both feet, the fighter lifts his hand from the ground and assumes a fighter's stance. He holds his hands high to protect his head and face. His fists are clenched, but relaxed. His elbows are close to his body, and his weight is evenly distributed on both feet, creating a stable base. He is light on his feet with his knees slightly flexed to allow quick movement in any direction.

Figure 3-7. The fighter's stance.

b. **Escape the Mount, Trap, and Roll**. This move starts with the fighter on his back and the enemy mounted on his chest.

(1) **Step 1** (Figure 3-8). Using both hands the fighter secures one of the enemy's arms and places his foot over the same side foot of the enemy, keeping his elbows tucked in as much as possible.

Figure 3-8. Escape the mount, trap, and roll, step 1.

(2) *Step 2* (Figure 3-9). The fighter now lifts the enemy straight up with his hips and, because the enemy has neither a hand nor a foot to stop him, he will topple over.

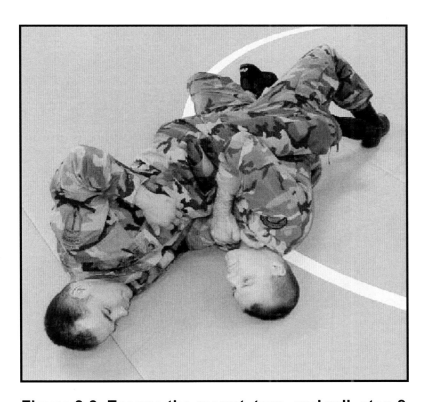

Figure 3-9. Escape the mount, trap, and roll, step 2.

(3) **Step 3** (Figure 3-10). As the enemy begins to fall, the fighter turns over, ending within the enemy's guard.

Figure 3-10. Escape the mount, trap, and roll, step 3.

c. **Escape the Mount, Shrimp to the Guard.** This move also starts with the fighter on his back and the enemy mounted on his chest. While the fighter is attempting to escape the mount, trap, and roll, he may be unable to capture the enemy's leg. This occurs when the enemy moves his leg away. This movement, however, creates an opening under the same leg. The term shrimp refers to the action of moving the hips away, which is crucial to the success of this technique.

(1) **Step 1** (Figure 3-11). The fighter turns on his side and faces toward the opening created by the enemy, ensuring that his leg is flat on the ground.

Figure 3-11. Escape the mount, shrimp to the guard, step 1.

(2) *Step 2* (Figure 3-12). The fighter now uses either his elbow or hand to hold the enemy's leg in place and brings his knee through the opening.

Figure 3-12. Escape the mount, shrimp to the guard, step 2.

(3) *Step 3* (Figure 3-13). When his knee gets past the enemy's leg, the fighter places his weight on the same leg and turn towards the other side. This action will bring his knee up and create enough space to pull the leg out and place it over the enemy's leg.

Figure 3-13. Escape the mount, shrimp to the guard, step 3.

(4) *Step 4* (Figure 3-14). The fighter now uses his hands to hold the enemy's other leg in place to repeat the actions from the first side.

Figure 3-14. Escape the mount, shrimp to the guard, step 4.

(5) **Step 5** (Figure 3-15). It is important that the fighter lock his feet together around the enemy, placing him in the open guard.

Figure 3-15. Escape the mount, shrimp to the guard, step 5.

d. **Pass the Guard and Achieve the Mount.** The fighter is in base within the enemy's guard. From this position, the fighter must escape from within the enemy's legs. This action is called passing the guard.

(1) **Step 1** (Figure 3-16). The first thing the fighter must do is defend against the front choke by using one hand to pin one of the enemy's arms to the ground at the biceps. He also keeps an upright posture.

Figure 3-16. Pass the guard and achieve the mount, step 1.

(2) **Step 2** (Figure 3-17). The fighter then raises his opposite side foot and places it on the ground just out of reach of the enemy's hand. He turns his hips, creating an opening, and pushes his hand through, fingertips first.

Figure 3-17. Pass the guard and achieve the mount, step 2.

(3) **Step 3** (Figure 3-18). The fighter then slides down and back until the enemy's leg is on his shoulder.

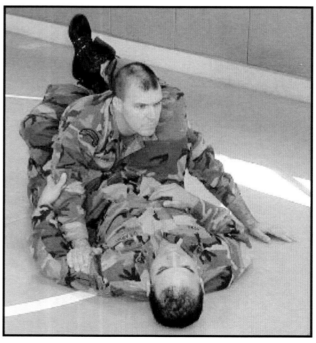

Figure 3-18. Pass the guard and achieve the mount, step 3.

(4) *Step 4* (Figure 3-19). With the same hand, the fighter grasps the enemy's collar with his thumb on the inside and drives the enemy's knee straight past his head. Pressure on the enemy's spine forces him to release his legs.

Figure 3-19. Pass the guard and achieve the mount, step 4.

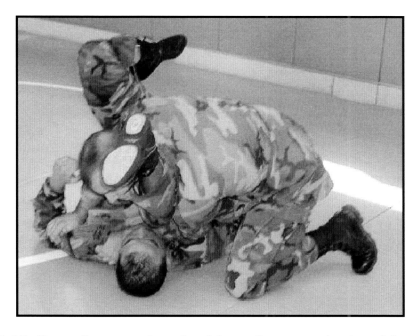

Figure 3-19. Pass the guard and achieve the mount, step 4 (continued).

(5) *Step 5* (Figure 3-20). The fighter rides the enemy down into side control.

Figure 3-20. Pass the guard and achieve the mount, step 5.

Figure 3-20. Pass the guard and achieve the mount, step 5 (continued).

(6) *Step 6* (Figure 3-21). The fighter faces toward the enemy's legs and changes his hips, ensuring that his knee is controlling the enemy's hip, and that his legs are spread out to avoid a reversal.

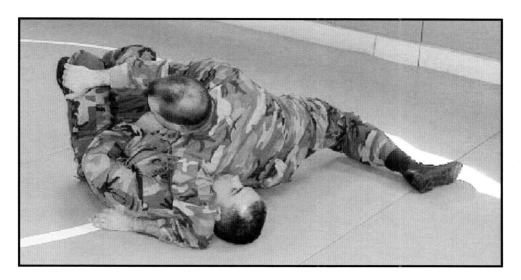

Figure 3-21. Pass the guard and achieve the mount, step 6.

(7) *Step 7* (Figure 3-22). The fighter uses his free hand to control the enemy's legs, and swings his leg over into the mount.

Figure 3-22. Pass the guard and achieve the mount, step 7.

e. **Escape the Half Guard.** Frequently the enemy will wrap his legs around one of fighter's from the bottom. This is called the half guard.

(1) *Step 1* (Figure 3-23). The fighter must prevent the enemy from either regaining the guard, or rolling him over. To do this, the fighter must assume a strong position. He should ensure that his elbow is against the side of the enemy's neck, and he is blocking the enemy from placing his leg under him with his bottom knee.

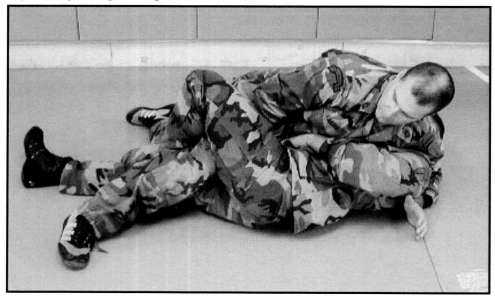

Figure 3-23. Escape the half guard, step 1.

(2) *Step 2* (Figure 3-24). By moving first the toe and then the heel of the captured foot, the fighter "walks" it closer to the enemy's buttocks.

Figure 3-24. Escape the half guard, step 2.

(3) *Step 3* (Figure 3-25). The fighter uses his free hand to push the enemy's knee until the fighter's knee is exposed, and then drives it over the enemy until it is on the ground.

Figure 3-25. Escape the half guard, step 3.

(4) *Step 4* (Figure 3-26). If the enemy attempts to push against the fighter's knee with his hand, the fighter places his hand under the enemy's arm at the bend in his elbow and pushes it upward towards his head.

Figure 3-26. Escape the half guard, step 4.

f. **Arm Push and Roll to the Rear Mount**. The fighter starts this technique in the front mount.

(1) *Step 1* (Figure 3-27). When the enemy attempts to protect his face from punches by crossing his arms over it, the fighter uses both hands to push one arm farther across and captures it in place by using his body weight.

Figure 3-27. Arm push and roll to the rear mount, step 1.

Figure 3-27. Arm push and roll to the rear mount, step 1 (continued).

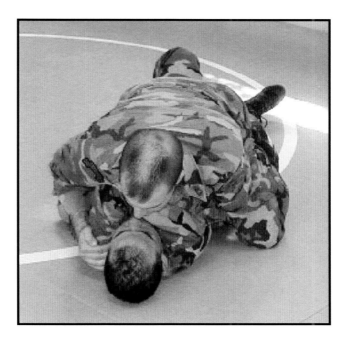

Figure 3-27. Arm push and roll to the rear mount, step 1 (continued).

(2) *Step 2* (Figure 3-28). While keeping control with one hand, the fighter uses the other hand to reach around the enemy's head and grasp the wrist of the captured hand.

Figure 3-28. Arm push and roll to the rear mount, step 2.

(3) *Step 3* (Figure 3-29). The fighter now places the first hand on the enemy's elbow and, by pushing with his chest, turns the enemy onto his stomach. The hand on the elbow is used to hold the enemy in place while the fighter repositions his chest for further pushing.

Figure 3-29. Arm push and roll to the rear mount, step 3.

(4) *Step 4* (Figure 3-30). The enemy will sometimes use his elbow as a post to avoid being turned to his stomach. When this happens, the fighter brings his weight slightly off of the enemy and uses his hand to pull the elbow under the enemy, pushing him forward onto his stomach.

Figure 3-30. Arm push and roll to the rear mount, step 4.

(5) *Step 5* (Figure 3-31). From this position the enemy normally tries to rise up and get his knees under him. When he attempts this, the fighter sits up and brings both legs around, "hooking" them inside of the enemy's legs, and grasps his hands together around the enemy's chest. One arm should be over the enemy's shoulder and the other should be under his arm.

Figure 3-31. Arm push and roll to the rear mount, step 5.

g. **Escape the Rear Mount.** This technique begins with the fighter face down and the enemy on the fighter's back in the rear mount.

(1) *Step 1* (Figure 3-32). The fighter must first roll over one shoulder so the enemy ends up underneath him, both facing skyward.

Figure 3-32. Escape the rear mount., step 1.

(2) **Step 2** (Figure 3-33). He now places one arm beside his own ear as shown and the other across his body in his armpit. This will prevent the enemy from securing a choke.

Figure 3-33. Escape the rear mount. step 2.

(3) **Step 3** (Figure 3-34). Falling toward the side of his own raised arm, the fighter pushes himself toward his own shoulders using the ground to "scrape " the enemy off his back.

Figure 3-34. Escape the rear mount, step 3.

(4) *Step 4* (Figure 3-35). Once his back is on the ground, the fighter uses his arms and legs to step over and gain the mount.

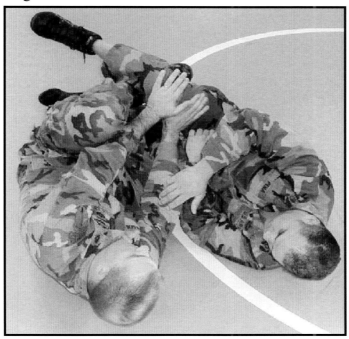

Figure 3-35. Escape the rear mount, step 4.

Figure 3-35. Escape the rear mount, step 4 (continued).

3-6. FINISHING MOVES

When dominant body position has been achieved the fighter can attempt to finish the fight secure in the knowledge that if an attempt fails, as long as he maintains dominant position, he may simply try again.

a. **Rear Naked Choke.** Chokes are the most effective method of disabling an enemy. This technique should only be executed from the back mount after both leg hooks are in place.

(1) *Step 1* (Figure 3-36). Leaving the weak hand in place, the fighter reaches around the enemy's neck and under his chin with the strong hand.

Figure 3-36. Rear naked choke, step 1.

(2) **Step 2** (Figure 3-37). The fighter now places the biceps of the weak hand under the strong hand, moves the weak hand to the back of the enemy's head, and completes the choke by expanding his chest.

Figure 3-37. Rear naked choke, step 2.

b. **Cross Collar Choke from the Mount and Guard.** This technique can only be executed from the guard or the mount.

(1) *Step 1* (Figure 3-38). With the weak hand, the fighter grasps the enemy's collar and pulls it open.

Figure 3-38. Cross collar choke from the mount, step 1.

(2) *Step 2* (Figure 3-39). While keeping a hold with the weak hand, the fighter now inserts his strong hand, fingers first, onto the collar. The hand should be relaxed and reach around to the back of the neck grasping the collar.

Figure 3-39. Cross collar choke from the mount, step 2.

(3) **Step 3** (Figure 3-40). After grasping the back of the enemy's collar, the fighter inserts the weak hand under the strong hand and into the collar, fingers first, touching or very close to the first hand.

Figure 3-40. Cross collar choke from the mount, step 3.

(4) **Step 4** (Figure 3-41). The fighter turns his wrists so that the palms face toward him, and brings his elbows to his side. He will complete the choke by expanding his chest and pulling with the muscles of his back.

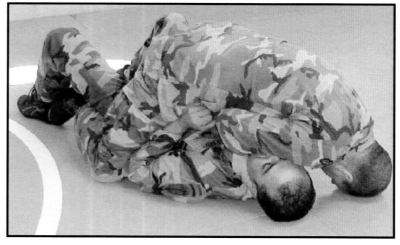

Figure 3-41. Cross collar choke from the mount, step 4.

Note: If the fighter is applying this choke from the mount, he should put his head on the ground on the side of the top hand and relax into the choke.

    c. **Front Guillotine Choke.** Many times this technique may be used as a counter to the double leg takedown.

    (1) *Step 1* (Figure 3-42). As the enemy shoots in toward the fighter's legs, the fighter should ensure that the enemy's head goes underneath one of his arms. The fighter wraps his arm around the enemy's head and under his neck. The fighter's palm should be facing his own chest.

Figure 3-42. Front guillotine choke, step 1.

(2) **Step 2** (Figure 3-43). With the other hand, the fighter grasps the first hand, ensuring that he has not reached around the enemy's arm, and pulls upward with both hands.

Figure 3-43. Front guillotine choke, step 2.

(3) *Step 3* (Figure 3-44). He now sits down and places the enemy within his guard, and finishes the choke by pulling with his arms and pushing with his legs.

Figure 3-44. Front guillotine choke, step 3.

d. **Bent Arm Bar from the Mount and Cross Mount.**

(1) *Step 1* (Figure 3-45). When the fighter has mounted the enemy, the enemy may try to cover his face by putting both arms up. Using the heel of his hand, the fighter drives the enemy's wrist to the ground ensuring that his elbow goes to the elbow notch (elbow between collarbone and the head with pressure against the neck).

Figure 3-45. Bent arm bar from the mount and cross mount, step 1.

Figure 3-45. Bent arm bar from the mount and cross mount, step 1 (continued).

(2) *Step 2* (Figure 3-46). With the other hand, the fighter reaches under the enemy's bent arm and grasps his own wrist.

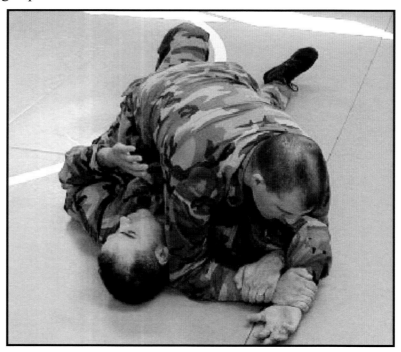

Figure 3-46. Bent arm bar from the mount and cross mount, step 2.

(3) *Step 3* (Figure 3-47). The fighter raises the enemy's elbow and at the same time drags the back of his hand along the ground like a paint brush, breaking the enemy's arm at the shoulder.

Figure 3-47. Bent arm bar from the mount and cross mount, step 3.

e. **Straight Arm Bar from the Mount.**

(1) *Step 1* (Figure 3-48). From the mount, the enemy may attempt to push the fighter off with his arms. The fighter places both of his arms on the enemy's chest ensuring that his arm goes over the targeted arm.

Figure 3-48. Straight arm bar from the mount, step 1.

(2) *Step 2* (Figure 3-49). Placing all of his weight on the enemy's chest, the fighter pops up and places his feet under him, ensuring that he keeps his butt low.

Figure 3-49. Straight arm bar from the mount, step 2.

(3) *Step 3* (Figure 3-50). Keeping his weight on the enemy's chest, he now swings his leg around and over the enemy's head and slides down the arm.

Figure 3-50. Straight arm bar from the mount, step 3.

(4) **Step 4** (Figure 3-51). The fighter now pinches the enemy's arm between his legs, grasps the arm at the wrist, and falls back extending the arm. The breaking action is hip pressure against the elbow joint.

Figure 3-51. Straight arm bar from the mount, step 4.

f.   **Straight Arm Bar from the Guard.**

(1) **Step 1** (Figure 3-52). When the fighter is on his back with the enemy in his guard, the enemy will sometimes present a straight arm such as when trying to choke. The fighter should secure the target arm above the shoulder.

Figure 3-52. Straight arm bar from the guard, step 1.

(2) *Step 2* (Figure 3-53). The fighter inserts his other hand under the enemy's leg on the side opposite the targeted arm. The hand should be palm up.

Figure 3-53. Straight arm bar from the guard, step 2.

(3) *Step 3* (Figure 3-54). By releasing his legs from around the enemy's waist and raising them above him, the fighter changes his center of gravity.

Figure 3-54. Straight arm bar from the guard, step 3.

(4) *Step 4* (Figure 3-55). He now curls his back to give himself a point on which to spin, and by pulling with the arm on the side opposite the targeted arm, he spins around and places his leg over the enemy's head, capturing the target arm between his legs.

Figure 3-55. Straight arm bar from the guard, step 4.

(5) *Step 5* (Figure 3-56). The fighter now brings his hand from under the enemy's leg and secures the wrist of the targeted arm, completing the move by breaking the targeted arm with pressure from his hips.

Figure 3-56. Straight arm bar from the guard, step 5.

g. **Sweep from the Attempted Straight Arm Bar.**

(1) *Step 1* (Figure 3-57). If the enemy tucks his head in to avoid the arm bar, The fighter maintains his grip on the enemy's leg and swings his own leg down to gain momentum. The fighter ensures that he curls his leg under after swinging it down.

Figure 3-57. Sweep from the attempted straight arm bar, step 1.

(2) *Step 2* (Figure 3-58, continued on page 3-40). The fighter pushes the enemy straight over with his other leg and finishes mounted.

Figure 3-58. Sweep from the attempted straight arm bar, step 2.

Figure 3-58. Sweep from the attempted straight arm bar, step 2 (continued).

3-7. DRILLS

Drills are used as a portion of the warm-up, which allows the maximum use of training time, stresses the importance of position, and also keeps training focused on perfecting the basic moves. Different details can be taught or emphasized during each training session. This will result in a deeper understanding of the techniques, as well as building muscle memory, teaching the soldiers to move in the most efficient ways naturally. More advanced techniques can be substituted within the framework of the drill after sufficient skill level is shown in the basics.

a. **Drill 1 (Basic Drill).** This drill begins with one soldier mounted.

(1) *Step 1.* The soldier on the bottom escapes the mount using the trap and roll technique.

(2) *Step 2.* The same soldier passes the guard and achieves the mount.

(3) *Step 3.* The roles now reverse and the second soldier goes through steps one and two.

b. **Drill 2.** This drill also begins with one soldier mounted.

(1) *Step 1.* Using the arm trap and roll technique, the soldier on top gains the back mount.

(2) *Step 2.* As soon as the first soldier sets the hooks in, the second soldier rolls over one shoulder and escapes the back mount.

(3) *Step 3.* When the second soldier is mounted, the roles will reverse, and they will go back through steps one and two.

3-8. DEFENSE AGAINST HEADLOCKS
The headlock is a very poor technique for anything more than immobilizing an enemy. It is, however, a very common technique in actual fighting; therefore, knowing how to escape is very important for a soldier. The techniques are progressive, and should be attempted in the order taught.

a. **Form the Frame.**

(1) *Step 1* (Figure 3-59). The fighter's first step in escaping from a headlock is to ensure that his arm is not captured. With a short jerky motion, the fighter pulls his elbow in and turns on his side.

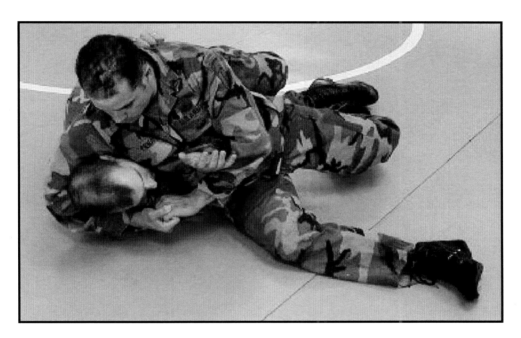

Figure 3-59. Form the frame, step 1.

(2) *Step 2* (Figure 3-60). If able, the fighter forms a frame under the enemy's chin. The fighter's top arm should be under the enemy's jawbone, and his top hand should rest comfortably in the grasp of the other hand. At this point, the fighter's bone structure should be supporting the enemy's weight.

Figure 3-60. Form the frame, step 2.

(3) *Step 3* (Figure 3-61). By pushing with the top leg, the fighter moves his hips back away from the enemy.

Figure 3-61. Form the frame, step 3.

(4) **Step 4** (Figure 3-62). The fighter reaches with both legs to grasp the enemy's head. If the enemy lets go of his headlock, the fighter squeezes the enemy's neck with his legs.

Figure 3-62. Form the frame, step 4.

(5) **Step 5** (Figure 3-63). If the enemy does not release the headlock, the fighter rotates around until he is on both of his knees behind the enemy's back.

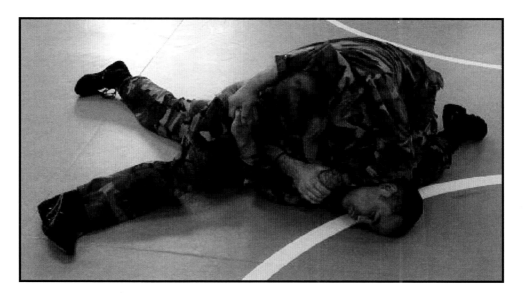

Figure 3-63. Form the frame, step 5.

(6) **Step 6** (Figure 3-64). The fighter uses his top hand to clear the enemy's legs out of the way and steps over, bringing his foot in tight against the enemy's hip. The fighter establishes his base by putting both hands on the ground.

Figure 3-64. Form the frame, step 6.

Figure 3-64. Form the frame, step 6 (continued).

(7) *Step 7* (Figure 3-65). The fighter forces the enemy to release his grip on the fighter's neck by forming the frame and leaning toward the enemy's head, driving the bone of his upper arm under the enemy's jawbone.

Figure 3-65. Form the frame, step 7.

b. **Follow the Leg.** Although the fighter should always try to form the frame, sometimes the enemy will tuck his head in making it impossible.

(1) *Step 1* (Figure 3-66). After ensuring that his arm is not captured as in the first technique, the fighter moves as close to the enemy as possible and places his leg over him. The fighter's heel should find the crease at the enemy's hip formed by his leg.

Figure 3-66. Follow the leg, step 1.

(2) *Step 2* (Figure 3-67). The fighter pulls his bottom arm free and places his weight on it. Holding the enemy tightly at the other shoulder, the fighter crawls over him using his own leg as a guide.

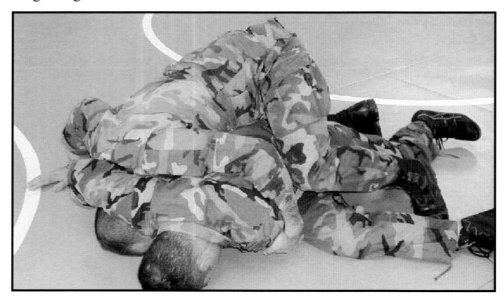

Figure 3-67. Follow the leg, step 2.

(3) *Step 3* (Figure 3-68). At this point the enemy has the option to either roll with the fighter or not. If he does not, the fighter uses all of his body to apply pressure to the enemy's shoulder. This will break the enemy's grip and leave the fighter behind the enemy. If the enemy rolls with the fighter, the fighter brings his foot into the enemy's hip as before and break his grip by forming the frame and applying pressure toward his head.

Figure 3-68. Follow the leg, step 3.

c. **Roll Toward the Head** (Figure 3-69). If the enemy should succeed in capturing the fighter's arm, the fighter can use the enemy's reaction to his attempts to free it to his advantage. With short jerky motions, the fighter attempts to pull his arm free. The enemy will have to adjust his position by leaning toward the fighter. Immediately after the fighter attempts to pull his arm free and feels the enemy pushing, the fighter arches toward his head and then over his opposite shoulder, taking the enemy over.

Figure 3-69. Roll toward the head.

Figure 3-69. Roll toward the head (continued).

Note: The roll must be timed correctly and must be toward the fighter's head and not straight over his body.

CHAPTER 4
ADVANCED GROUND-FIGHTING TECHNIQUES

After achieving an understanding of the basics of ground fighting, other elements of fighting on the ground are added. These techniques, however, are dependent on a thorough grasp of the basics. Being systematic is important in building competent fighters. Staying with the program will not only produce competent fighters quickly, but will produce the most competent fighters over time as well.

Section I. ADVANCED ATTACKS

Concentrating on offensive techniques is preferable when developing a training plan. The best defense is simply knowing that the technique exists. If defenses are to be taught, there should be ample time between teaching the offense and teaching the defense to allow time for the students to master the offensive skills first. Training the defense prematurely will hinder development.

4-1. ADVANCED BODY POSITIONS

a. **North-South Position** (Figure 4-1). This position allows many possible attacks and is very difficult for the enemy to escape from. You should attempt to control the enemy's arms by placing your elbows on the ground in his arm pits. You will also need to shift your weight in order to prevent him from rolling you over.

Figure 4-1. North-south position.

b. **Knee in the Stomach** (Figure 4-2). Another very important dominant body position is the knee mount. When in the knee mount, the knee should be in the middle of the enemy's chest. The foot should be hooked around his hip. The opposite knee should be off of the ground and back away from the enemy's head, and the hips should be set forward to maintain balance.

Figure 4-2. Knee in the stomach.

4-2. PASS THE GUARD

When you are inside of the enemy's guard, he has many options to attack you or reverse the positions. Therefore, you will need several possible techniques to pass.

a. **Closed Guard.** In the closed guard, the enemy has his legs locked together behind your back.

(1) *Knee in the Tailbone.*

(a) *Step 1* (Figure 4-3). Moving one hand at a time, grasp the enemy at the belt with both hands. Keep pressure on him to prevent him from sitting up.

Figure 4-3. Knee in the tailbone, step 1.

(b) *Step 2* (Figure 4-4). Place one of your knees in the enemy's tailbone. You will need to lean toward the other side to prevent him from compromising your balance.

Figure 4-4. Knee in the tailbone, step 2.

(c) *Step 3* (Figure 4-5). Push with both hands, and move your other knee back away from him. This should create a 90 degree angle from the knee in the tailbone. This action will also create more distance between the knee in the tailbone and your hip, forcing him to loosen the grip with his legs.

Figure 4-5. Knee in the tailbone, step 3.

(d) *Step 4* (Figure 4-6). Release your grip with the hand on the side you are facing and move it under the enemy's leg on the same side. You will then lift his leg, pulling it to you to gain control, and pass normally.

Figure 4-6. Knee in the tailbone, step 4.

Figure 4-6. Knee in the tailbone, step 4 (continued).

e. *Step 5* (Figure 4-7). Pull your remaining hand out from between his legs at the earliest possible time to avoid the arm bar, and secure a grip at his waist.

Figure 4-7. Knee in the tailbone, step 5.

(2) **_Stand Up With One Sleeve._**

(a) *Step 1* (Figure 4-8). Gain control of one of the enemy's sleeves near the wrist, and with the other hand grasp his jacket in the center to keep him from sitting up.

Figure 4-8. Stand up with one sleeve, step 1.

(b) *Step 2* (Figure 4-9). Stand up with the leg closest to the arm you are controlling first and arch your back slightly, pulling on the sleeve that you control.

Figure 4-9. Stand up with one sleeve, step 2.

Figure 4-9. Stand up with one sleeve, step 2 (continued).

(c) *Step 3* (Figure 4-10). Switch control of his sleeve to your other hand and use the original hand to push downward on his legs to break his grip. It is helpful to step slightly back with the leg on the side you are attempting to open.

Figure 4-10. Stand up with one sleeve, step 3.

(d) *Step 4* (Figure 4-11). When his grip breaks, reach under the leg and pull it to you, tightening up to gain control and pass like before. It is important to control the leg below his knee so that he cannot bend it to escape and regain the guard.

Figure 4-11. Stand up with one sleeve, step 3.

(3) *Hands in the Arm Pits.*

(a) *Step 1* (Figure 4-12). Pin the enemy's shoulders to the ground by either placing the fingers of your hands in both of his armpits, or placing both hands around his neck.

Figure 4-12. Hands in the arm pits, step 1.

Figure 4-12. Hands in the arm pits, step 1 (continued).

(b) *Step 2* (Figure 4-13). Stand up one leg at a time, placing one of your knees in his tailbone and stepping back with the other. The heal of your foot must be planted on the ground.

Figure 4-13. Hands in the arm pits, step 2.

(c) *Step 3* (Figure 4-14). Sit down so that your knee is driven upward between the enemy's legs. This will break the grip of his legs behind your back.

Figure 4-14. Hands in the arm pits, step 3.

(d) *Step 4* (Figure 4-15). Drive your knee over his leg on the opposite side. This will immobilize the leg so that you can bring both legs over into side control.

Figure 4-15. Hands in the arm pits, step 4.

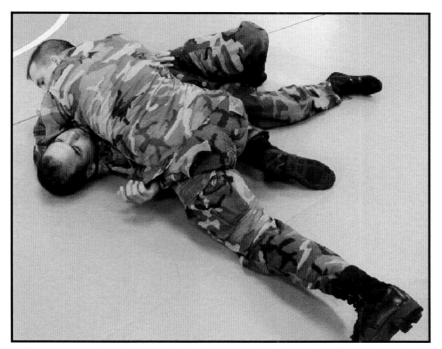

Figure 4-15. Hands in the arm pits, step 4 (continued).

b. **Open Guard.** Once you have opened the enemy's guard, he may block your passing by controlling you with his legs. You must gain control of his legs before you can pass.

(1) *Throw the Legs.*

(a) *Step 1* (Figure 4-16). Grasp the enemy's pant legs near the ankles with a firm grasp and stand up, pulling him slightly toward you.

Figure 4-16. Throw the legs, step 1.

(b) *Step 2* (Figure 4-17). Swing both legs from side to side and then throw them forcefully to one side.

Figure 4-17. Throw the legs, step 2.

(c) *Step 3* (Figure 4-18). Close the distance and gain control in either the side control or knee mount position.

Figure 4-18. Throw the legs, step 3.

(2) *Push the Knees.*
(a) *Step 1* (Figure 4-19). Gain control of the enemy's pant legs on top of each knee.

Figure 4-19. Push the knees, step 1.

(b) *Step 2* (Figure 4-20). Step back and drive both knees downward.

Figure 4-20. Push the knees, step 2.

(c) *Step 3* (Figure 4-21). While still holding the enemy's knees down, jump forward with both legs into the mounted position.

Figure 4-21. Push the knees, step 3.

4-3.   ATTACKS FROM THE MOUNT

After the mount has been achieved, there are many options on how to attack. The first is to throw punches into the enemy's face and force him to turn over, giving up his back. If he does not turn over he will most likely give an opening, making the following attacks easier.

a.   **Chokes.** The most efficient way to incapacitate an enemy is to choke him into unconsciousness. An advantage of prioritizing chokes in training is that they can be applied in training exactly as applied in combat.

(1) *Paper Cutter Choke.*

(a) *Step 1* (Figure 4-22). Start by opening the collar with the weak hand, as in the cross collar choke. With the strong hand grasp deep into the collar, inserting the thumb on the inside.

Figure 4-22. Paper cutter choke, step 1.

(b) *Step 2* (Figure 4-23). Release the grip of the first hand and grasp the opposite side of the enemy's jacket, pulling it tight against the back of his neck.

Figure 4-23. Paper cutter choke, step 2.

(c) *Step 3* (Figure 4-24). Drive the elbow of the other hand across the enemy's neck to complete the choke.

Figure 4-24. Paper cutter choke, step 3.

(2) *Leaning Choke.*

(a) *Step 1* (Figure 4-25). Grasp both sides of the collar. The knuckles should be pointed inward and there should be three or four inches of slack.

Figure 4-25. Leaning choke, step 1.

(b) *Step 2* (Figure 4-26). Pull one side of the collar across the enemy's neck so the pinky knuckle is just past the Adam's apple where the blood vessels are located. Pull the other hand tight as you drive this hand into the enemy's neck.

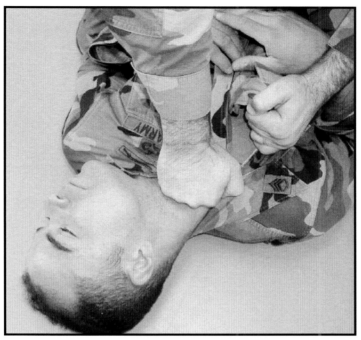

Figure 4-26. Leaning choke, step 2.

(3) *Nutcracker Choke.*

(a) *Step 1* (Figure 4-27). Grasp the collar with both hands at the sides of the enemy's neck. Knuckles should be pointed in against the neck.

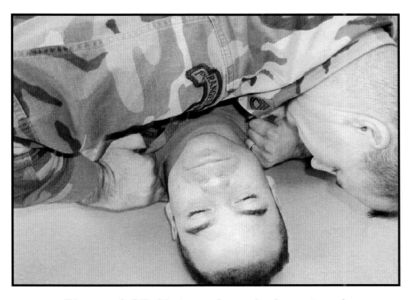

Figure 4-27. Nutcracker choke, step 1.

(b) *Step 2* (Figure 4-28). Pull the collar tight against the back of the enemy's neck with both hands and, with the pinkies acting as the base, drive the pointer finger knuckles of both hands into the enemy's neck on either side of the Adam's apple.

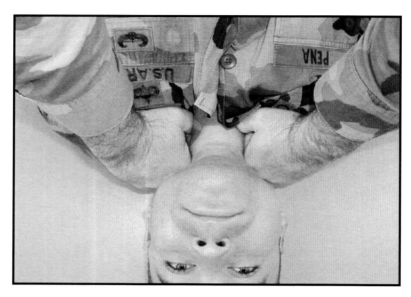

Figure 4-28. Nutcracker choke, step 2.

(4) *Sleeve Choke.*

(a) *Step 1* (Figure 4-29). Place the fingers of one hand inside the sleeve cuff of the other with a firm grip.

Figure 4-29. Sleeve choke, step 1.

(b) *Step 2* (Figure 4-30). Drive the other hand behind the enemy's head so the forearm of the first hand goes across the neck.

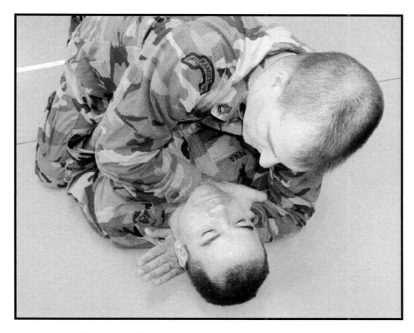

Figure 4-30. Sleeve choke, step 2.

(c) *Step 3* (Figure 4-31). Drive the elbow across the enemy's neck toward the back while pulling with the other hand.

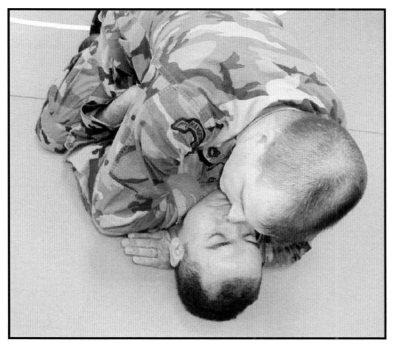

Figure 4-31. Sleeve choke, step 3.

b. **Triple Attack.** When the enemy tries to escape the mount using the trap and roll technique, he can be moved into the position shown by sliding the trapped foot forward and lifting on the enemy's opposite shoulder. This position presents several attack opportunities.

(1) *Lapel Choke.*

(a) *Step 1* (Figure 4-32). With the hand that corresponds to the side the enemy is facing, place the fingers inside of the enemy's collar and pull it open.

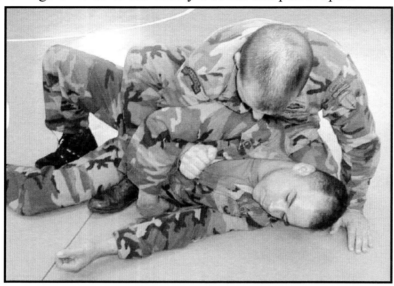

Figure 4-32. Lapel choke, step 1.

(b) *Step 2* (Figure 4-33). Reach under his head with the other hand and insert the thumb as deep as possible into the collar.

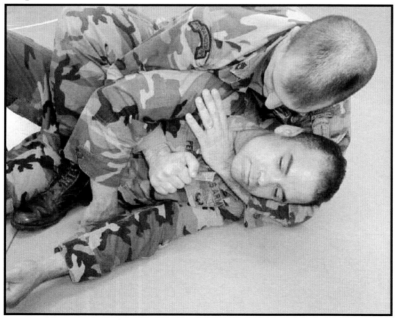

Figure 4-33. Lapel choke, step 2.

(c) *Step 3* (Figure 4-34). Change the grip of the first hand to the opposite side of his lapel to tighten the collar against the back of his neck.

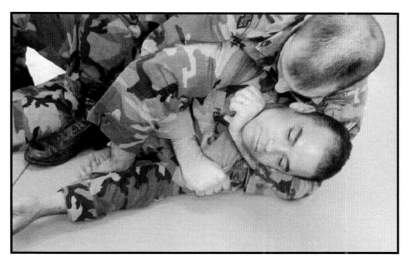

Figure 4-34. Lapel choke, step 3.

(d) *Step 4* (Figure 4-35). Tighten by extending both arms.

Figure 4-35. Lapel choke, step 4.

(2) **Straight Arm Bar.** The enemy may attempt to block the choke with his hands.

(a) *Step 1* (Figure 4-36). Ensuring that your arm is under the enemy's arm, push his elbow forward and hold it in place by grasping your own collar.

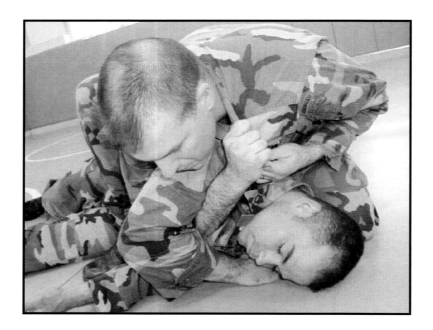

Figure 4-36. Straight arm bar, step 1.

(b) *Step 2* (Figure 4-37). Place your other hand on the enemy's head.

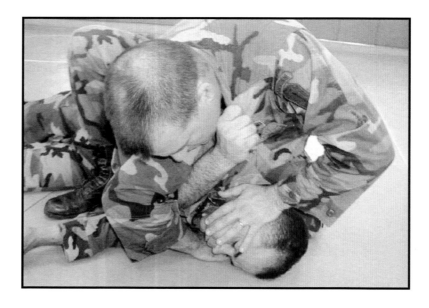

Figure 4-37. Straight arm bar, step 2.

(c) *Step 3* (Figure 4-38). Rest all of your weight on the enemy's head, and point your toe straight back.

Figure 4-38. Straight arm bar, step 3.

(d) *Step 4* (Figure 4-39). Swing your leg around on top of his head and sit back into the straight arm bar.

Figure 4-39. Straight arm bar, step 4.

(3) **Gain the Back Mount.** If the enemy defends both the choke and the arm bar, you still have another option.

(a) *Step 1* (Figure 4-40). Push the enemy toward his stomach with chest pressure, and at the same time bring your foot close to the enemy's back.

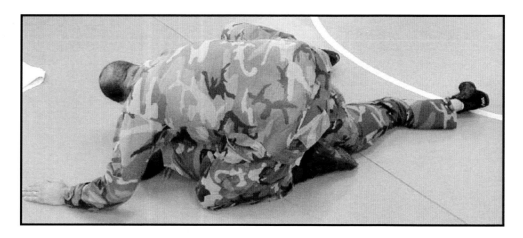

Figure 4-40. Gain the back mount, step 1.

(b) *Step 2* (Figure 4-41). Sit back, pulling the enemy on top of you, ensuring you give yourself room to swing your foot around to sink in your hook. You will finish in the back mount.

Figure 4-41. Gain the back mount, step 2.

4-4. ATTACKS FROM THE BACK MOUNT

Once the back mount has been achieved, keeping it is the most important goal. The position learned earlier of one hand in the armpit and the other over the opposite shoulder allows the most possible attacks.

a. **Collar Choke.**

(1) *Step 1* (Figure 4-42). Grasp the collar with the hand in the armpit, pulling it open to insert the thumb of the other hand deep into the collar. Secure a firm grip.

Figure 4-42. Collar choke, step 1.

(2) **Step 2** (Figure 4-43). Change the grip of the hand under the armpit to grasp the opposite lapel, pulling down to tighten the collar against the back of the enemy's neck.

Figure 4-43. Collar choke, step 2.

(3) **Step 3** (Figure 4-44). Set the choke by pushing outward with both hands.

Figure 4-44. Collar choke, step 3.

b. **Single Wing Choke.**

(1) **Step 1** (Figure 4-45). Open the collar and secure a grip the same as in the collar choke.

Figure 4-45. Single wing choke, step 1.

(2) **Step 2** (Figure 4-46). With the hand that is under the enemy's armpit, pull his arm out at the elbow.

Figure 4-46. Single wing choke, step 2.

(3) *Step 3* (Figure 4-47). Bring your hand around behind his head and finish the choke by pushing out with both hands.

Figure 4-47. Single wing choke, step 3.

c. **Straight Arm Bar.**

(1) *Step 1* (Figure 4-48). If the enemy is protecting his collar effectively, push your arm further through his armpit, pulling your own collar open with the other hand. Grasp your collar with the hand that is through his armpit.

Figure 4-48. Straight arm bar, step 1.

(2) **Step 2** (Figure 4-49). With the palm of your other hand, push his head away and step your leg over it. Break his grip by pushing with your legs and extending your body.

Figure 4-49. Straight arm bar, step 2.

(3) **Step 3** (Figure 4-50). Finish with hip pressure against his elbow as in the basic straight arm bar.

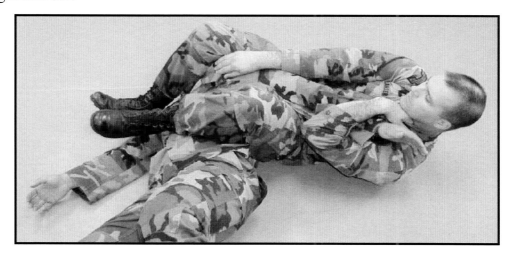

Figure 4-50. Straight arm bar, step 3.

4-5. ATTACKS FROM THE GUARD

a. **Arm Lock.**

(1) *Step 1* (Figure 4-51). If the enemy places his hand on the ground, grasp it around the wrist.

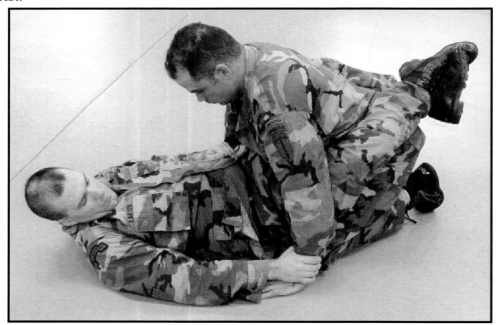

Figure 4-51. Arm lock, step 1.

(2) *Step 2* (Figure 4-52). Release your legs and sit up. Reach over and around his arm grasping your own wrist.

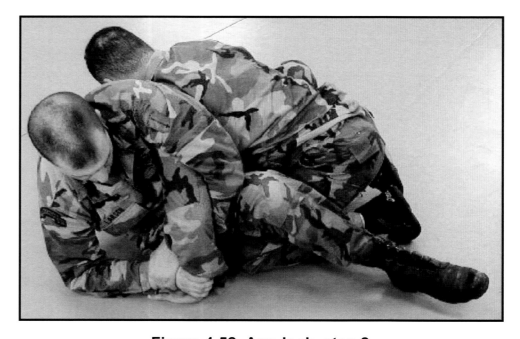

Figure 4-52. Arm lock, step 2.

(3) **Step 3** (Figure 4-53). Keep your legs tight against his sides to prevent him stepping over them, and sit back.

Figure 4-53. Arm lock, step 3.

(4) **Step 4** (Figure 4-54). Move your hips out from under him and finish by rotating your torso to attack his shoulder joint. Ensure that his arm is held at 90 degrees and not up behind his back.

Figure 4-54. Arm lock, step 4.

b. **Guillotine Choke.** When you are attempting the arm bar, the enemy may try to counter by grasping you around the waist.

(1) *Step 1* (Figure 4-55). Release your grasp of his wrist and place your hand on the ground behind you. This allows you to move your hips back until you are sitting straight up.

Figure 4-55. Guillotine choke, step 1.

(2) *Step 2* (Figure 4-56). Wrap your other hand around the enemy's neck and under his chin. Grasp his chin with the hand that was on the ground. Both palms should be facing your body.

Figure 4-56. Guillotine choke, step 2.

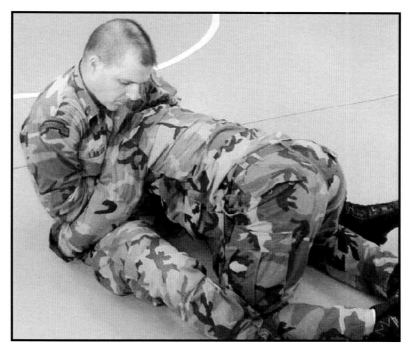

Figure 4-56. Guillotine choke, step 2 (continued).

(3) *Step 3* (Figure 4-57). Pull upward with both hands and finish the choke by leaning backwards and wrapping your legs around him, pull with your arms and push with your legs.

Figure 4-57. Guillotine choke, step 3.

c. **Sweeps.** When you have the enemy within your guard, he may provide the chance to reverse the positions.

(1) *Scissors Sweep.*

(a) *Step 1* (Figure 4-58). When the enemy raises one leg while attempting to pass the guard, you should place your weight on the calf on that side and swing your hips out from underneath him. Your leg should go along his belt line with your foot hooked around his waist.

Figure 4-58. Scissors sweep, step 1.

Figure 4-58. Scissors sweep, step 1 (continued).

(b) *Step 2* (Figure 4-59). Move your chest away and kick him over with a scissors action from your legs, ending up mounted.

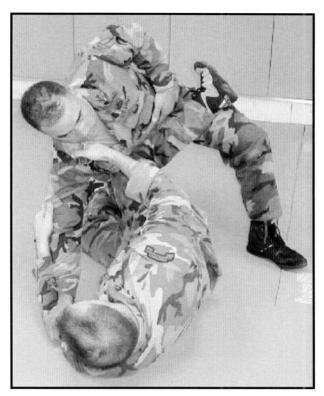

Figure 4-59. Scissors sweep, step 2.

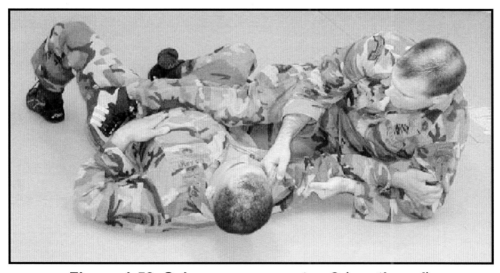

Figure 4-59. Scissors sweep, step 2 (continued).

(2) *Captain Kirk.* The enemy may attempt to pass by standing up. When he does he is very susceptible to being swept.

(a) *Step 1* (Figure 4-60). When the enemy stands up, maintain control with your arms and let your feet slide naturally down until they are on his hips.

Figure 4-60. Captain Kirk, step 1.

(b) *Step 2* (Figure 4-61). If his weight gets too far forward, pick him up with your legs and throw him over one of your shoulders. Ensure that you move your head to the opposite side to prevent him landing on you. Finish mounted.

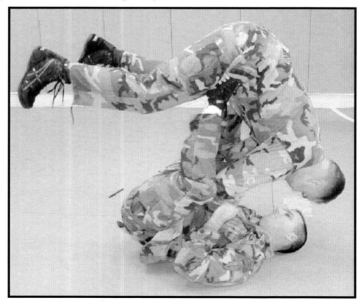

Figure 4-61. Captain Kirk, step 2.

(3) *Ankle Grab/Knee Push.*

(a) *Step 1* (Figure 4-62). When the enemy stands up, maintain control with your arms and let your feet slide to his hips as in the previous move.

Figure 4-62. Ankle grab/knee push, step 1.

(b) *Step 2* (Figure 4-63). If his weight gets too far back, let go with your arms and grasp both of his ankles. Push your knees upward causing him to fall backwards.

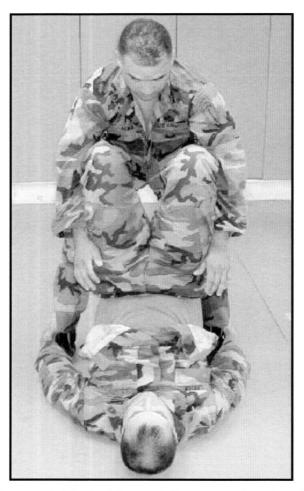

Figure 4-63. Ankle grab/knee push, step 2.

Figure 4-63. Ankle grab/knee push, step 2 (continued).

(c) *Step 3* (Figure 4-64). Drive one of your knees to the ground and grasp the back of his neck with the other hand to pull yourself to the mount.

Figure 4-64. Ankle grab/knee push, step 3.

d. **Triangle Choke.** If the enemy gets his hand through and begins to pass your guard, you still have a chance to apply a choke.

(1) *Step 1* (Figure 4-65). Post your leg on the ground and turn your body perpendicular to the enemy's. Your leg should be around the back of his neck.

Figure 4-65. Triangle choke, step 1.

(2) *Step 2* (Figure 4-66). Place the inside of your knee over your own foot. You may assist yourself by grasping your foot with your hand.

Figure 4-66. Triangle choke, step 2.

(3) *Step 3* (Figure 4-67). Place both of your hands on the back of the enemy's head and push upward with your hips.

Figure 4-67. Triangle choke, step 3.

4-6. KNEE MOUNT

When the enemy is defending well from side control, a good option is to go to the knee mount.

a. Achieve the knee mount from standard side control.

(1) *Step 1* (Figure 4-68). With the hand closest to the enemy's head, grasp the collar on either side of his head.

Figure 4-68. Knee mount from standard side control, step 1.

(2) *Step 2* (Figure 4-69). With the other hand, grasp his belt or his uniform over his hip.

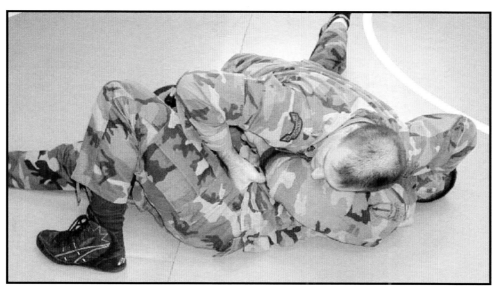

Figure 4-69. Knee mount from standard side control, step 2.

(3) **Step 3** (Figure 4-70). Pushing up with both hands, pop up into the knee mount with one swift movement.

Figure 4-70. Knee mount from standard side control, step 3.

b. Achieve the knee mount with control of the far side arm.

(1) **Step 1** (Figure 4-71). From side control, move your arm through the enemy's armpit.

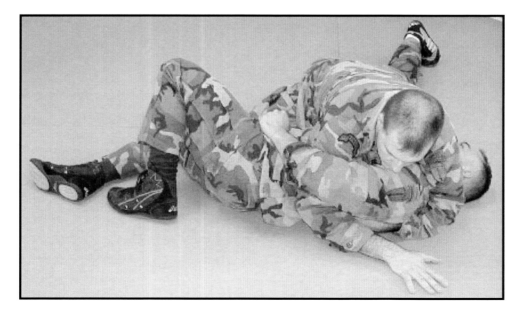

Figure 4-71. Achieve knee mount with control of far side arm, step 1.

(2) **Step 2** (Figure 4-72). With the other arm, reach back and gain control of his elbow. Pulling the arm upwards as you change your hips, sit through to the position shown.

Figure 4-72. Achieve knee mount with control of far side arm, step 2.

Figure 4-72. Achieve knee mount with control of far side arm, step 2 (continued).

(3) *Step 3* (Figure 4-73). Place the foot of the leg closest to the enemy underneath the other leg. With your weight on the hand in the enemy's armpit and your outside leg, swing your inside leg up into the knee mount. Ensure that you maintain control of the enemy's near side arm.

Figure 4-73. Achieve knee mount with control of far side arm, step 3.

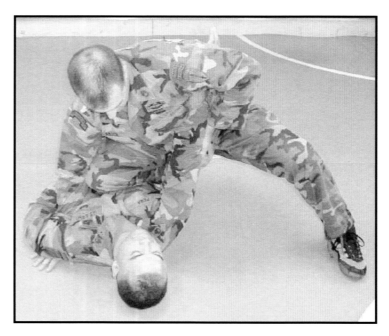

Figure 4-73. Achieve knee mount with control of far side arm, step 3 (continued).

c. **Attacks from the Knee Mount.**

(1) *Chokes with Hand on the Far Side of the Enemy's Neck.*

(a) *Step 1* (Figure 4-74). If the enemy does not defend against chokes, reach under the first arm and grasp well down into the collar with your fingers inside the collar.

Figure 4-74. Choke from the knee mount with hand on far side of enemy's neck, step 1.

(b) *Step 2* (Figure 4-75). Bring your knee back off of the enemy's chest, placing it to control his hip, and finish as in the paper cutter choke.

Figure 4-75. Choke from the knee mount with hand on far side of enemy's neck, step 2.

(2) *Chokes with Hand on the Near Side of the Enemy's Neck.*

(a) *Step 1* (Figure 4-76). Reach into the far side of the enemy's collar with your fingers on the inside of the collar.

Figure 4-76. Choke from the knee mount with hand on near side of enemy's neck, step 1.

(b) *Step 2* (Figure 4-77). With your weight on the leg closest to his head, sit through and drive your elbow across his neck.

Figure 4-77. Choke from the knee mount with hand on near side of enemy's neck, step 2.

(3) *Straight Arm Bar from the Knee Mount.*

(a) *Step 1* (Figure 4-78). If the enemy pushes up with his near side arm, grasp it at the elbow with your arm closest to the enemy's head. Step over his head with the same side leg.

Figure 4-78. Straight arm bar from the knee mount, step 1.

Figure 4-78. Straight arm bar from the knee mount, step 1 (continued).

(b) *Step 2* (Figure 4-79). Sit down as close to his shoulder as possible and lay back into the straight arm bar. You may need to twist slightly toward his legs because the change in your leg position allows him an opportunity to roll out of the technique. You do not need to bring your other leg across his body.

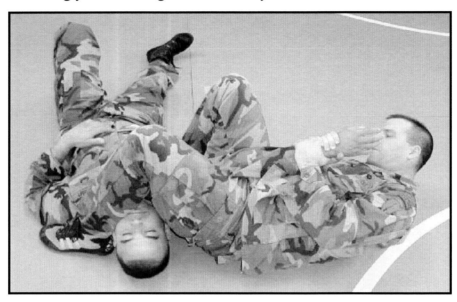

Figure 4-79. Straight arm bar from the knee mount, step 2.

(4) *Bent Arm Bar from the Knee Mount.*

(a) *Step 1* (Figure 4-80). If the enemy tries to push your knee off, grasp his wrist with the hand closest to his legs.

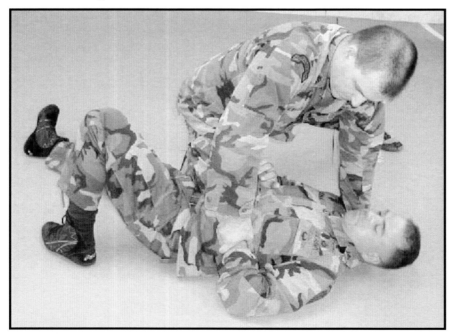

Figure 4-80. Bent arm bar from the knee mount, step 1.

(b) *Step 2* (Figure 4-81). Back your knee off of his chest and reach over his arm with the other hand, grasping your own wrist. Your second hand should be wrapped completely around his arm at this time.

Figure 4-81. Bent arm bar from the knee mount, step 2.

(c) *Step 3* (Figure 4-82). Move around until his head is between your knees, and pull him up onto his side.

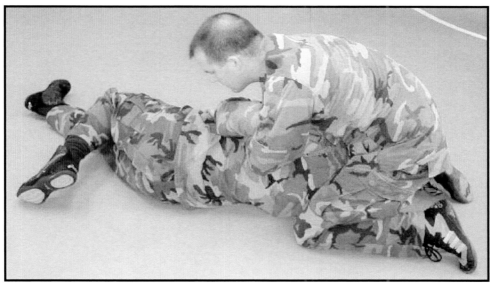

Figure 4-82. Bent arm bar from the knee mount, step 3.

(d) *Step 4* (Figure 4-83). Break his grip by pulling his arm quickly toward his head.

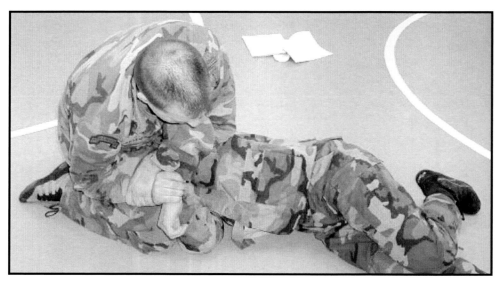

Figure 4-83. Bent arm bar from the knee mount, step 4.

(e) *Step 5* (Figure 4-84). Step your foot into the small of his back, and break his shoulder by rotating your torso towards his back.

Figure 4-84. Bent arm bar from the knee mount, step 5.

Note: It is important to keep the enemy's elbow tight to your chest to keep him from escaping.

(5) *Variation of Straight Arm Bar from the Knee Mount.*

(a) *Step 1* (Figure 4-85). If the enemy has a firm grip and you cannot get the bent arm bar, push your arm farther through and grasp your own lapel.

Figure 4-85. Variation of the straight arm bar from the knee mount, step 1.

(b) *Step 2* (Figure 4-86). Stand up and place your foot over his head and in front of his chin.

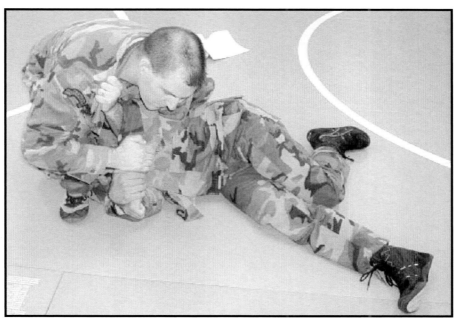

Figure 4-86. Variation of the straight arm bar from the knee mount, step 2.

4-7. LEG ATTACKS

Leg attacks, although very effective, have the drawback of giving up dominant body position. Therefore, they are not the preferred method of attack. Soldiers must be familiar with them or they will fall easy prey to them. As in all attacks, knowing the technique exists is the primary defense.

a. **Straight Ankle Lock.**

(1) *Step 1* (Figure 4-87). When you are trying to pass the enemy's open guard, you may catch his foot in your armpit. Wrap your arm around his leg and squat down, ensuring that your opposite side knee comes up between his legs.

Figure 4-87. Straight ankle lock, step 1.

(2) *Step 2* (Figure 4-88). Push away from the enemy, ensuring that you allow his leg to slide through your grip until you are holding around his ankle.

Figure 4-88. Straight ankle lock, step 2.

(3) *Step 3* (Figure 4-89). Bring your outside foot up to push the enemy's torso back, preventing him from sitting up to counter the lock. Form a figure four on his ankle and finish the break by arching your back.

Figure 4-89. Straight ankle lock, step 3.

b. **Figure-Four Ankle Lock** (Figure 4-90). You are on top of the enemy in the north-south position. The enemy may bring his knee up in order to defend against your attacks or attempt to strike you. When he does, reach under his leg from the outside, near the ankle. With the other hand, grasp his foot and form the figure four as shown with the first hand. Apply pressure to break the enemy's foot.

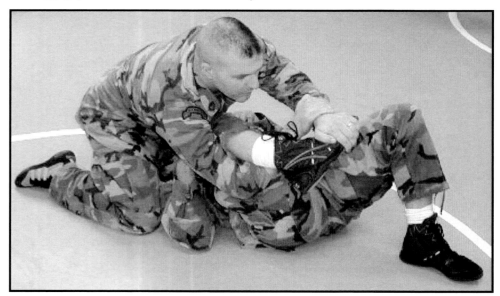

Figure 4-90. Figure-four ankle lock.

c. **Straight Knee Bar.**

(1) *Step 1* (Figure 4-91). The enemy is beneath you and has one of your legs between his. Reach your arm under his far side leg, stand up, and step over his body with your other leg.

Figure 4-91. Straight knee bar, step 1.

Figure 4-91. Straight knee bar, step 1 (continued).

(2) *Step 2* (Figure 4-92). Keep your hips as close to the enemy's as possible and lock your legs behind his buttocks. Break the knee with hip pressure just as in a straight arm bar. You may also place his leg into your armpit to increase the pressure, or switch to the figure-four ankle lock at any time.

Figure 4-92. Straight knee bar, step 2.

Figure 4-92. Straight knee bar, step 2 (continued).

Section II. STRIKES

Striking is an integral part of all actual fighting. Practicing ground-fighting techniques exclusively without strikes is a common mistake.

4-8. PASS THE GUARD WITH STRIKES

a. **Step 1** (Figure 4-93). Keeping your head close to the enemy's chest, drive both hands up the center of his body and then out to control his arms at the biceps.

Figure 4-93. Pass the guard with strikes, step 1.

b. **Step 2** (Figure 4-94). Give the enemy a couple of head butts.

Figure 4-94. Pass the guard with strikes, step 2.

Note: Ensure that head butts are not given with the center of the forehead, which could result in injuring your own nose.

c. **Step 3** (Figure 4-95). Stand up one leg at a time, and change your grip to one hand on the jacket. Your hips should be pushed slightly forward.

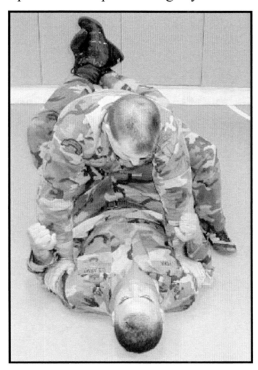

Figure 4-95. Pass the guard with strikes, step 3.

Figure 4-95. Pass the guard with strikes, step 3 (continued).

d. **Step 4** (Figure 4-96). With your free hand, strike the enemy a couple of times in the head.

Figure 4-96. Pass the guard with strikes, step 4.

(At this point the enemy may release the grip with his legs. If he does, step 5 is as follows.)

e. **Step 5** (Figure 4-97). Press inward with your knees. This will cause his legs to stick out so that you can reach behind one of them. Gain control of the leg and pass normally.

Figure 4-97. Pass the guard with strikes, step 5.

Figure 4-97. Pass the guard with strikes, step 5 (continued).

(If he does not release his legs, step 5 is as follows.)

f. **Step 5 (Alternate)** (Figure 4-98). While he is distracted by your strikes, step back with one leg and push your hand through the opening. Place your hand on your own knee and squat down to break the grip of his legs. Gain control of his leg and pass normally.

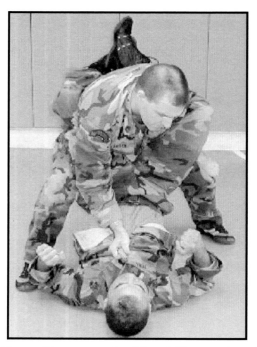

Figure 4-98. Pass the guard with strikes, step 5 (alternate).

Figure 4-98. Pass the guard with strikes, step 5 (alternate) (continued).

4-9.   STRIKING FROM SIDE CONTROL

The goal of striking while ground fighting is to improve your position or create an opening for a better attack. In this case you would most likely be trying to mount.

a.   **Step 1** (Figure 4-99). Keeping your head low so that the enemy will not be able to knee you in the head, move your hand that is closest to the enemy's legs into his armpit.

Figure 4-99. Striking from side control, step 1.

b.   **Step 2** (Figure 4-100). Move your other arm around his head and clasp your hands together. Lean your shoulder onto his head to keep his chin pointed away from you. This will make it more difficult for him to turn his body toward you to regain the guard.

Figure 4-100. Striking from side control, step 2.

c. **Step 3** (Figure 4-101). Move your leg that is closer to his head into his armpit, driving his arm upwards until it is pinched against his head between your arm and leg.

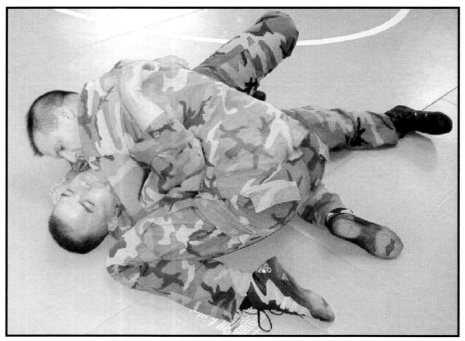

Figure 4-101. Striking from side control, step 3.

d. **Step 4** (Figure 4-102). Point the toes of your other foot toward the sky and drive your knee into his ribs.

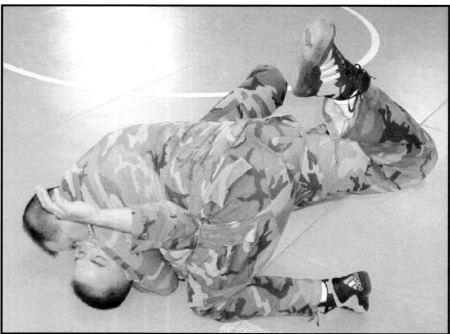

Figure 4-102 Striking from side control, step 4.

e. **Step 5** (Figure 4-103). When he changes his position to defend against your strikes, step over and gain the mounted position.

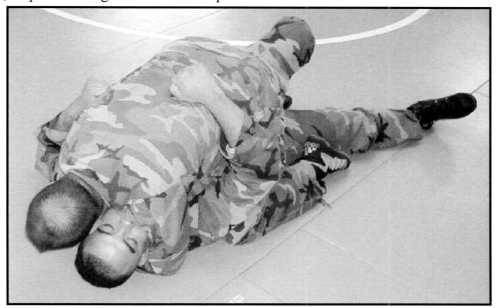

Figure 4-103. Striking from side control, step 5.

4-10. DEFENDING AGAINST STRIKES IN THE GUARD

As with standup fighting, the best method to avoid punches is to stay very close to the enemy. Controlling the range is the key.

a. **Step 1** (Figure 4-104). Pull the enemy into your closed guard and grasp him around the neck. One hand should be pushing his head and the other should be pulling it to defend against head butts and punches. Tuck your head in and control his punches with your elbows.

Figure 4-104. Defending against strikes in the guard, step 1.

b. **Step 2** (Figure 4-105). The enemy will eventually become frustrated by his inability to land solid blows and will attempt to pull away. When he does so, slide your arms over his triceps and your feet to his hips. Control his punches with your knees. As he struggles to gain a position to strike from, you will have to continuously regain this position.

Figure 4-105. Defending against strikes in the guard, step 2.

c. **Step 3** (Figure 4-106). Your hands are placed over the enemy's triceps to keep him from getting his arms loose for big punches. He may however be able to free one of his arms. If he does so and attempts to land a big punch, push your knee toward the loose arm to extend the distance and reach to the inside of his punching arm. This will avoid the strike and allow you to regain control of his arm.

Figure 4-106. Defending against strikes in the guard, step 3.

d. **Step 4** (Figure 4-107). The enemy may attempt to stand up. When he does you should sit up toward him, and when you have enough space to do so safely, stand up in base. You may need to use a kick with your bottom leg to create enough space.

Figure 4-107. Defending against strikes in the guard, step 4.

CHAPTER 5
TAKEDOWNS AND THROWS

Before progressing into takedowns and throws, soldiers must learn how to fall to the ground without getting hurt, both during training and during combat. Each practice repetition of a throw or takedown is a chance for the training partner to perfect his breakfalls.

5-1. BREAKFALLS

The most important point during breakfall training is to not try to catch yourself by reaching out with your arms, but to take the impact of the fall on the meaty portions of the body. After initial training on breakfalls has been conducted, it must be followed up with refresher breakfall training before training on throws and takedowns. This can be accomplished easily by making it part of your warm-up.

a. **Side Breakfall Position** (Figure 5-1). Before training on breakfalls can take place, soldiers must understand the basic breakfall position. Laying on his left side, the soldier extends his left leg and bends his right leg, raising his right leg off the ground. His left arm is extended, palm down, slightly away from his side. His right arm is bent in front of his face to defend against attacks. This should be practiced on both sides.

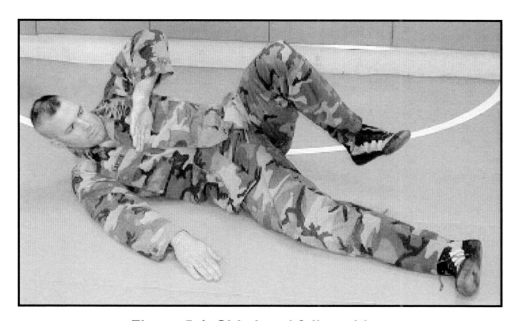

Figure 5-1. Side breakfall position.

b. **Forward Rolling Breakfall from the Kneeling Position.** After soldiers are familiar with the side breakfall position, the best way to introduce them to the mechanics of falling is by starting them on their knees.

(1) **Step 1** (Figure 5-2). The fighter assumes a kneeling posture with his left arm raised in the air. He places his left arm across the front of his body, palm down, outside of his right knee.

Figure 5-2. Forward rolling breakfall from the kneeling position, step 1.

Figure 5-2. Forward rolling breakfall from the kneeling position, step 1 (continued).

(2) *Step 2* (Figure 5-3). He rolls over his left shoulder, along his arm, landing on his right side with his right leg extended in the right side breakfall position.

Figure 5-3. Forward rolling breakfall from the kneeling position, step 2.

c. **Forward Rolling Breakfall** (Figure 5-4). When soldiers have mastered the forward rolling breakfall from the kneeling position, they will progress to the standing position.

(1) *Step 1*. The soldier starts the fall from the standing position. He raises one arm to expose his entire side, places both hands on the ground, and bends both knees.

(2) *Step 2.* He rolls forward across the body along the hand, arm, and back to the opposite hip.

(3) *Step 3.* He ends in a good side breakfall position.

Figure 5-4. Forward rolling fall.

d. **Rear Breakfall** (Figure 5-5). There are also many times when a fighter will take a fall straight down to his back.

(1) *Step 1.* The fighter starts the fall from the standing position and keeps his head forward to reduce the chance of head and neck injuries.

(2) *Step 2.* He then falls backward and lowers his center of gravity by bending both knees. As his buttocks touch the ground, he rolls backward to absorb the momentum of the fall.

(3) *Step 3.* He keeps his hands cupped and slaps his hands and arms down to help absorb the shock of impact and to stabilize his body.

Figure 5-5. Rear breakfall.

5-2. CLOSING THE DISTANCE AND ACHIEVING THE CLINCH

Controlling a standup fight means controlling the range between fighters. The untrained fighter is primarily dangerous at punching range. The goal is to avoid that range. Even if you are the superior striker, the most dangerous thing you can do is to spend time at the range where the enemy has the highest probability of victory. When training soldiers, the primary goal should be instilling the courage to close the distance. Recognizing that standup fighting skills are difficult to master in a short amount of time, compare takedowns to the basic tackle. The following techniques are essentially a more sophisticated way to tackle the enemy.

a. **The Clinch.** The clinch position is the optimum way to hold an enemy after you have successfully closed the distance, but have not yet executed a successful takedown. While in the clinch, you have control of the enemy's far side arm at the elbow, with the arm also tucked into your armpit. Your head is tucked into the enemy's chest, and you hand is around his waist, controlling his hip. Your legs are sufficiently back to prevent him from getting his hips under you to attempt a throw. There are two ranges where confrontations start.

(1) *Close Range.* This occurs when the enemy is within striking range.

(a) *Step 1* (Figure 5-6). When a confrontation seems likely, you will face the potential enemy and bring your hands up in a non-threatening manner.

(b) *Step 2* (Figure 5-7). When the enemy attacks, change levels by pulling both feet up and placing them out in a broad stance. Simultaneously bring both arms up to cover the most dangerous possible attacks. It is important not to anticipate the means of attack, but to cover for the most dangerous potential attacks. Therefore both arms should come up every time.

Figure 5-6. The clinch, step 1.

Figure 5-7. The clinch, step 2.

(c) *Step 3* (Figure 5-8). To clinch, reach over the far side arm and pull it down into your armpit, controlling it at the elbow. Simultaneously step around to the other side and drive your other elbow under his arm until you can reach around his waist and achieve the clinch.

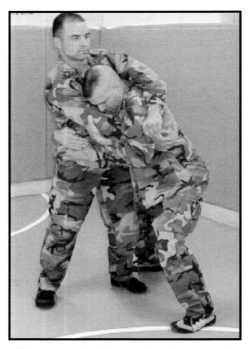

Figure 5-8. The clinch, step 3.

(2) ***Long Range.*** It is more common for a confrontation to start outside of striking range. Having the courage to close the distance is the principle training goal.

(a) *Basic Long Range.* From a fighter's stance, at an opportune moment, drive into the enemy. Try to place your forehead on his chest. You should keep your head up so that your forehead is pointed at the enemy and your hands should go just over his biceps. From this position, achieve the clinch as before.

(b) *Long Range when the Enemy Attacks.* If the enemy tries to initiate the attack with punches, use this opportunity to close the distance. He will be closing the distance to get into punching range, therefore clinching will be that much easier.

(c) *Long Range with a Kick.* If the enemy is content to stand back and await your attack, you will need to gain some form of advantage before closing the distance. One way to do this is with a kick. The kick should be with the front leg, and should be aimed at the enemy's thigh. It is important that if you miss the kick, your leg should fall in front of the enemy so that you do not give up your back.

5-3.   THROWS AND TAKEDOWNS

All of the throws and takedowns in this section assume that you have already achieved the clinch. It is important to remember that most sport-type throws are executed at what, in a real fight, would be striking range.

    a. **Basic Takedown.** This is the basic tackle.

    (1) *Step 1* (Figure 5-9). From the clinch, step slightly to the front of the enemy and change your grip. Both palms are pointed down and your hands are at the enemy's kidneys.

Figure 5-9. Basic takedown, step 1.

    (2) *Step 2* (Figure 5-10). Pulling with your hands and pushing with your head and shoulder, break the enemy's balance to the rear.

Figure 5-10. Basic takedown, step 2.

(3) *Step 3* (Figure 5-11). Step over the enemy and release your grip, ending in the mounted position.

Figure 5-11. Basic takedown, step 3.

Note: It is very important to release your hands to avoid landing on them.

b. **Hook the Leg** (Figure 5-12). If the enemy attempts to pull away, use your leg closest to his back to hook his leg. When he begins to fall, release the leg and finish as before.

Figure 5-12. Hook the leg.

c. **Hip Throw.** The enemy may attempt to avoid the tackle by leaning forward.

(1) *Step 1* (Figure 5-13). With the leg that is behind the enemy, step through until you are standing in front of him with your legs inside of his. Your hip should be pushed well through.

Figure 5-13. Hip throw, step 1.

(2) *Step 2* (Figure 5-14). Using a scooping motion with your hips, lift the enemy and throw him over your hip. You should land in the knee mount or side control.

Figure 5-14. Hip throw, step 2.

Figure 5-14. Hip throw, step 2 (continued).

d. **Rear Takedown** (Figure 5-15). Frequently, you will end up after the clinch with your head behind the enemy's arm. When this happens, you grasp your hands together around his waist by interlocking your fingers, and place your forehead in the middle of the small of his back to avoid strikes. From this secure position, you can attempt to take the enemy down.

Figure 5-15. Rear takedown.

(1) **Step 1** (Figure 5-16). Step to one side so that you are behind the enemy at an angle.

Figure 5-16. Rear takedown, step 1.

(2) **Step 2** (Figure 5-17). With the leg that is behind the enemy, reach out and place the instep of your foot behind the enemy's far side foot so that he cannot step backward. Sit down as close to your other foot as possible and hang your weight from the enemy's waist.

Figure 5-17. Rear takedown, step 2

(3) *Step 3* (Figure 5-18). The enemy will fall backwards over your extended leg. As he does so, tuck your elbow in to avoid falling on it, and rotate up into the mounted position.

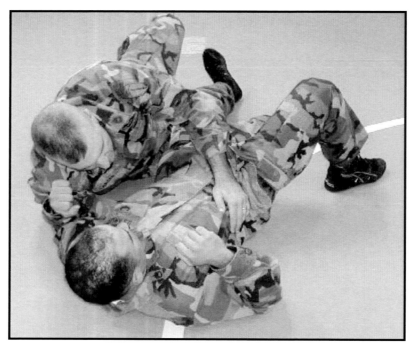

Figure 5-18. Rear takedown, step 3.

Figure 5-18. Rear takedown, step 3 (continued).

5-4. DEFENDING AGAINST HEADLOCKS

a. **Defend the Guillotine.**

(1) *Step 1* (Figure 5-19). When you find yourself caught in the guillotine choke, reach over the enemy's opposite shoulder with your arm. Turn your head slightly inward and grasp the enemy's wrist to help alleviate the pressure. You should also relax and hang as dead weight. If the enemy is taller than you, place your knees on his thighs to support you.

Figure 5-19. Defend the guillotine, step 1.

(2) *Step 2* (Figure 5-20). As the enemy tries to pick you up to choke you, bounce around to the opposite side from the choke. Break his base by bumping the back of his knee with your knee, and lower him carefully to the ground. Ensure that you are in side control as you set him down.

Figure 5-20. Defend the guillotine, step 2.

Figure 5-20. Defend the guillotine, step 2 (continued).

Figure 5-20. Defend the guillotine, step 2 (continued).

(3) **Step 3** (Figure 5-21). With the hand that is closest to his head, grasp his far side shoulder and drive the bony portion of your forearm under his chin until you can pull your head free.

Figure 5-21. Defend the guillotine, step 3.

b. **Defend the Guillotine with Knee Strikes.** When the enemy has secured the guillotine choke, he may attempt to direct knee strikes to your head.

(1) **Step 1** (Figure 5-22). With both arms locked out at the elbows, and the heels of the hands together, block the enemy's knee strikes just above the knee. It is very important that your thumbs be alongside your hands so that they are not broken by the enemy's knee strikes. Your leg that is on the side corresponding with the side of the enemy that your head is on, should be forward, and the other leg back. Your leg that is on the same side of the enemy as your head should be forward, and your other leg back.

Figure 5-22. Defend the guillotine with knee strikes, step 1.

(2) *Step 2* (Figure 5-23). Swing your back leg forward, between the enemy's legs, and sit down on your other heel. This dropping action will send the enemy over your head, driving his head into the ground.

Figure 5-23. Defend the guillotine with knee strikes, step 2.

Figure 5-23. Defend the guillotine with knee strikes, step 2 (continued).

> **CAUTION**
> This technique can be very dangerous to practice. It should always be practiced with the enemy's outside hand free, allowing him to roll out. Soldiers should be proficient in rolling breakfalls, and great care must be taken to ensure they know how to properly roll out while practicing (Figure 5-24).

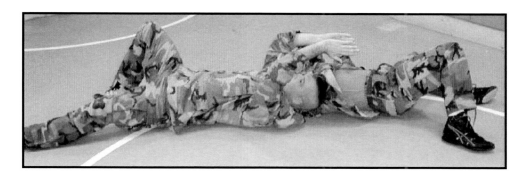

Figure 5-24. Defend the guillotine with knee strikes, caution.

c. **Headlock with Punches.** When you are behind the enemy and he has control of your head, He must release one of his hands in order to punch.

(1) *Step 1* (Figure 5-25). With your front arm attempt to grasp the enemy's punching arm and push it back, feeding it to your other arm. Grasp it from behind his back at the elbow.

Figure 5-25. Headlock with punches, step 1.

(2) *Step 2* (Figure 5-26). When the punching arm has been controlled, secure a grip on the top of the hand that is around your head, and place your hip against the enemy's side. At the same time, step and look away from the enemy, extending your body to break his grip. Hip pressure will keep him from following.

Figure 5-26. Headlock with punches, step 2.

(3) *Step 3* (Figure 5-27). Keep his hand pressed tightly against your chest, and with the foot closest to him, step backwards to place yourself standing behind him with his hand still captured against your chest.

Figure 5-27. Headlock with punches, step 3.

Figure 5-27. Headlock with punches, step 3 (continued).

d. **Head Lock Without Punches.** When the enemy has control of your head, he will normally try to hold on with both hands.

(1) *Step 1* (Figure 5-28). Block potential knee strikes by placing the heel of one hand just above the opposite side knee. Reach the other hand around the enemy's back and secure a grip at the far side of his hip bone. Your legs should be back so that he cannot get his hip under you.

Figure 5-28. Headlock without punches, step 1.

(2) *Step 2* (Figure 5-29). Step slightly in front of the enemy, and then with your outside foot, step between the enemy's legs and sit down on your heel. This should be a spinning action, and as you drop between his legs, pull him with the hand that was on his hip. He will fall over you so that you can roll up into the mount.

Figure 5-29. Headlock without punches, step 2.

Figure 5-29. Headlock without punches, step 2 (continued).

Note: Ensure that you tuck your elbow in as he falls to avoid landing on it.

5-5. TAKEDOWNS FROM AGAINST A WALL

If you are having difficulty gaining control of the enemy, a good technique is to push him against a wall.

a. **Position and Strikes** (Figure 5-30). Push him against the wall with one shoulder. One arm should be around his waist, and the other one should be on the inside of his knee to deflect knee strikes to your groin. One of your legs should be back to push, and the other one should be inside of the enemy's knee to deflect knee strikes. From this position, you can deliver strikes to the enemy's ribs by turning your hand over and attacking with the knuckles. When he attempts to cover his ribs, with a sharp movement, push your shoulder into him to gain enough space to strike his head.

Figure 5-30. Position and strikes against the wall.

Figure 5-30. Position and strikes against the wall (continued).

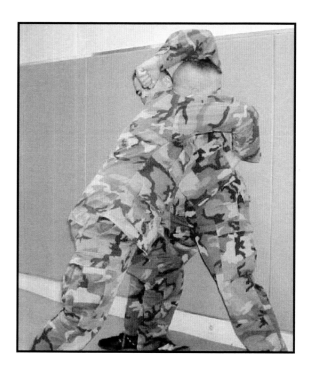

Figure 5-30. Position and strikes against the wall (continued).

Figure 5-30. Position and strikes against the wall (continued).

Figure 5-30. Position and strikes against the wall (continued).

b. **Leg Drag** (Figure 5-31). When the enemy attempts a knee strike on the side you are facing, capture his leg. Step back with the foot on the same side pulling him from the wall.

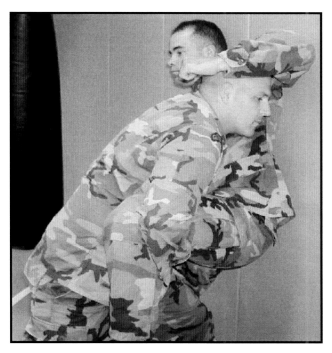

Figure 5-31. Leg drag.

Figure 5-31. Leg drag (continued).

5-6. DOUBLE LEG ATTACKS

Going under the enemy's arms and straight to the legs is a very useful type of attack. There are several ways to finish depending on the enemy's actions, but the initial attack is the same. When you find yourself relatively close to the enemy, change your level by bending both of your knees and drive into his midsection with your shoulder (Figure 5-32). One of your feet should penetrate as deep as the enemy's feet. Continue to drive and control the legs to end in side control.

Figure 5-32. Double leg attack.

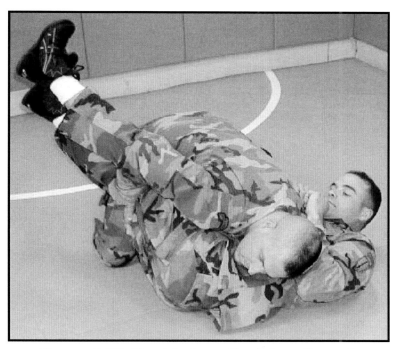

Figure 5-32. Double leg attack (continued).

a. **Finishes from the Double Leg Attack.**

(1) *Lift* (Figure 5-33). By driving your hips under him and arching your back, lift the enemy up. Push up with your head and, by controlling his legs with your arms, gain side control.

Figure 33. Lift.

Figure 33. Lift (continued).

Figure 33. Lift (continued).

Figure 33. Lift (continued).

b. **Hook the Leg** (Figure 5-34). Hook the enemy's heel with your outside leg and continue to drive through him.

Figure 5-34. Hook the leg.

5-7. SINGLE LEG ATTACKS

You may also choose to attack only one leg (Figure 5-35). Making a deep step with the inside leg, and reaching with the same side arm to the enemy's opposite knee, step to the outside and grasp your hands together behind his knee. Your head and shoulder should be tight against his thigh. Moves to finish a single leg attack include the dump, block the opposite knee, and the leg sweep.

Figure 5-35. Single leg attack.

Figure 5-35. Single leg attack (continued).

a. **Dump** (Figure 5-36). From the single leg position, with your shoulder tight against his thigh, take a short step in front of him, and then a longer step backward with your trail foot. Pressure from your head and shoulder will "dump" him on to his buttocks.

Figure 5-36. Dump.

Figure 5-36. Dump (continued).

b. **Block the Opposite Knee** (Figure 5-37). If the enemy turns away from you, maintain control of his leg and reach between his legs to block his opposite leg. Use pressure with your shoulder on the back of his leg to bring him face down on the ground.

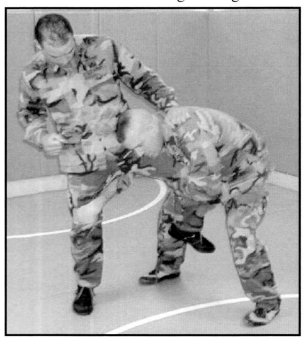

Figure 5-37. Block the opposite knee.

c. **Leg Sweep** (Figure 5-38). Reach your outside arm under his leg and with your outside hand reach down and gain control of his ankle. Pull his leg up with both of your arms and use your foot to sweep his post leg.

Figure 5-38. Leg sweep.

5-8.   ATTACK FROM THE REAR

In the rear attack, the unsuspecting is knocked to the ground and kicked in the groin, or rear mounted. The soldier can then kill the sentry by any proper means. Since surprise is the essential element of this technique, the soldier must use effective stalking techniques (Figure 5-39, Step 1). To initiate his attack, he grabs both of the sentry's ankles (Figure 5-39, Step 2). Then he heaves his body weight into the hips of the sentry while pulling up on the ankles. This technique slams the sentry to the ground on his face. Then, the soldier may follow with a kick to the groin (Figure 5-39, Step 3) or by achieving the rear mount.

Figure 5-39. Attack from the rear.

CHAPTER 6
STRIKES

Strikes are an inefficient method of ending a fight. However, they are a significant part of most fights, and a soldier must have an understanding of fighting at striking range. It is important to note that while at striking range, you are open to being struck. For this reason, it is often better to avoid striking range.

Section I. NATURAL WEAPONS

The key to developing effective striking skills is understanding range and knowing what techniques are effective at what range and controlling the transition between ranges. Techniques are taught individually, but they must be approached as a part of an overall fighting strategy. Effective striking is not something that can be taught overnight. This section describes natural weapon techniques of various punches, strikes, and kicks and addresses the ranges from which they are effective.

6-1. ARM STRIKES

The strikes in this section are presented individually. It is important to know that they will almost never be used this way. Follow-on sections will address combinations and how strikes fit into an overall fight strategy. Remember that when learning each of the following strikes to keep your guard up with the non-punching arm.

a. **Jab** (Figure 6-1). The jab is thrown with the lead hand and is used for controlling the range, and setting up further techniques. From the basic stance, snap your lead arm out with a slight pivot of your hip and shoulder. You should rotate your shoulder so that the punch lands with your palm down and quickly snap your arm back into the ready position. Your punch should travel in a straight line, and your elbow should never stick out away from your body at any time during the punch.

Figure 6-1. Jab.

Note: To step into your jab, drive off of your trail leg as you punch and slide your trail leg forward as you withdraw your punching arm.

b. **Reverse Punch** (Figure 6-2). The reverse punch is a power punch thrown from the rear arm. It can be a fight ender by itself, but it is also very useful to set up takedowns. From the basic stance, turn on the ball of your trail foot as if you were putting out a cigarette so that your hips and shoulders are facing toward the enemy. As you extend your punch, rotate your arm so that you strike with your knuckles up and palm facing down. You should extend your punch as if to go through your opponent and then snap back into the ready position.

Figure 6-2. Reverse punch.

Note: Ensure that you do not lock your elbow when your punch is fully extended.

c. **Hook** (Figure 6-3). The hook is a power punch that is usually thrown from the front arm. It is very powerful and works well in combinations. One of its main advantages is that it can be fully executed outside of the enemy's field of vision. The common mistake is to think of it as a looping arm punch. In reality a powerful hook does not involve very much arm movement, generating its power from your leg hip and shoulder movement. From the basic stance, turn on your lead foot as if you were putting out a cigarette, turning your hips and shoulders toward the inside. Raise your elbow as you turn so that your punch lands with your arm parallel with the ground, and your palm facing toward your chest. Your trail foot should remain planted. You should then smoothly tuck your elbow back in to your side and turn your shoulders to return to the ready position.

Figure 6-3. Hook.

d. **Uppercut.** The uppercut can be thrown with either hand and is particularly effective against an opponent who is crouching or trying to avoid a clinch.

(1) *Lead Hand Uppercut.*

(a) *Step 1* (Figure 6-4). From the basic stance, turn your hips and shoulders slightly to face the enemy, and dip your lead shoulder downward. You should be changing your level slightly by bending your knees.

Figure 6-4. Lead hand uppercut, step 1.

(b) *Step 2* (Figure 6-5). Keep your elbow tucked in and drive off of your lead leg to land your punch, palm facing up with your wrist firm and straight.

Figure 6-5. Lead hand uppercut, step 2.

(c) *Step 3.* Turn your shoulders and snap back into the ready position.
(2) ***Trail Hand Uppercut.***
(a) *Step 1* (Figure 6-6). From the basic stance, turn your hips and shoulders slightly to face the enemy, and dip your rear shoulder downward. You should be changing your level slightly by bending your knees.

Figure 6-6. Trail hand uppercut, step 1.

(b) *Step 2* (Figure 6-7). Drive off of your trail leg through your hip to land your punch, palm facing up with your wrist straight and firm. Your arm will be slightly more extended than the lead hand punch.

Figure 6-7. Trail hand uppercut, step 2.

(c) *Step 3.* Snap back into the ready position.

e. **Elbow Strikes.** Elbow strikes can be devastating blows and are very useful at close range. You should remember that they gain their power from the hips and legs.

(1) *Horizontal Elbow Strike* (Figure 6-8). A horizontal elbow strike is thrown almost exactly like a hook, with the exceptions that at the moment of impact the palm should be facing the ground.

Figure 6-8. Horizontal elbow strike.

(2) *Upward Elbow Strike* (Figure 6-9). The upward elbow strike is thrown almost exactly like an uppercut, with the exception that at the moment of impact the palm should be facing inward toward your head.

Figure 6-9. Upward elbow strike.

6-2. PUNCHING COMBINATIONS

Strikes must be thrown in combinations to be effective—"bunches of punches" as the old boxing saying goes. Combination punching must be practiced in order to come naturally while under the stress of combat. After the basic punches are learned individually, they should be practiced in combination. Particular attention should be paid to snapping each hand back into a defensive posture after it is used. Remember that when you are in punching range, so is the enemy. You must make a good defense an integral part of your offense. Some combination punches are:

*   Jab—reverse punch.
*   Jab—reverse punch—hook.
*   Jab—hook.
*   Jab—hook—reverse punch.
*   Lead hand uppercut to the body—trail hand uppercut to the body—hook to the head.
*   Lead hand uppercut to the body—trail hand uppercut to the body—lead hand horizontal elbow strike—trail hand upward elbow strike.

6-3. KICKS

Kicks during hand-to-hand combat are best directed at low targets and should be simple but effective. Combat soldiers are usually burdened with combat boots and LCE. His flexibility level is usually low during combat, and if engaged in hand-to-hand combat, he will be under high stress. He must rely on gross motor skills and kicks that do not require complicated movement or much training and practice to execute.

a. **Lead Leg Front Kick** (Figure 6-10). The lead leg front kick is not a very powerful kick, but it can be a very good tool to help control the range. The target should be the enemy's thigh, just above the knee. The striking surface is the sole of the foot. It is very important that if the kick does not land, your foot should not slide off toward the enemy's back. This would present your back to him.

Figure 6-10. Lead leg front kick.

b. **Rear Leg Front Kick** (Figure 6-11). The rear leg front kick is a much more powerful kick. The best target is the abdomen. The striking surface should be either the ball of the foot or the entire sole of the foot.

Figure 6-11. Rear leg front kick.

c. **Shin Kick**. The shin kick is a powerful kick, and it is easily performed with little training. When the legs are targeted, the kick is hard to defend against (Figure 6-12), and an opponent can be dropped by it.

Figure 6-12. Shin kick to the outer thigh.

d. **Stepping Side Kick** (Figure 6-13). A soldier starts a stepping side kick (Step 1) by stepping either behind or in front of his other foot to close the distance between him and his opponent. The movement is like that in a skip. The soldier now brings the knee of his kicking foot up and thrusts out a sidekick (Step 2). Tremendous power and momentum can be developed in this kick.

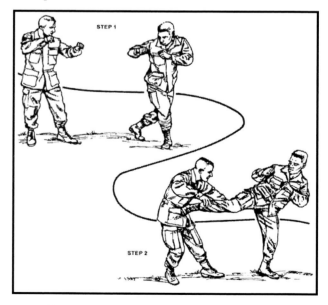

Figure 6-13. Stepping side kick.

e. **Knee Strike** (Figure 6-14). A knee strike can be a devastating weapon. It is best used when in the clinch, at very close range, or when the enemy is against a wall. The best target is the head, but the thigh or body may also be targeted under certain conditions.

Figure 6-14. Knee strike.

6-4. TRANSITION BETWEEN RANGES

In order to dominate the standup fight, you must be able to control the range between you and the enemy, and to operate effectively at the various ranges, keeping the enemy reacting to your techniques, and setting the pace of the fight. The ability to keep your head and continue to execute effective techniques requires practice. This is the heart of standup fighting. To transition between ranges, use a combination of techniques such as:

- Jab—reverse punch—shin kick to the outer thigh.
- Jab—reverse punch—shin kick to the outer thigh—high single leg takedown.

CHAPTER 7
HANDHELD WEAPONS

Handheld weapons provide a significant advantage during a fight. For soldiers to be well trained in their use there must be connectivity between the techniques of armed and unarmed fighting. As soldiers progress in their training, bayonet fighting techniques that are taught in initial entry training will merge with the other elements of hand-to-hand fighting to produce a soldier who is capable of operating across the full range of force.

Section I. OFFENSIVE TECHNIQUES

In most combat situations, small arms and grenades are the weapons of choice. However, in some scenarios, soldiers must engage the enemy in confined areas, such as trench clearing or room clearing or where noncombatants are present. In these instances, or when your primary weapon fails, the bayonet or knife may be the ideal weapon to dispatch the enemy. Soldiers must transition immediately and instinctively into the appropriate techniques based on the situation and the weapons at hand.

7-1. ANGLES OF ATTACK

Any attack, regardless of the type weapon, can be directed along one of nine angles of attack (Figure 7-1).

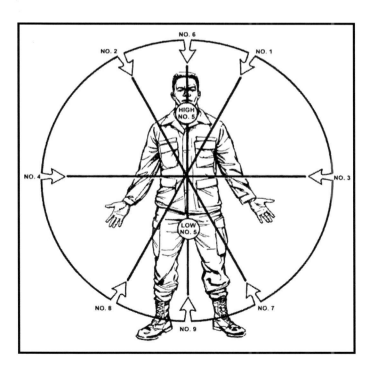

Figure 7-1. Angles of attack.

a. **No. 1 Angle of Attack.** A downward diagonal slash, stab, or strike toward the left side of the defender's head, neck, or torso.

b. **No. 2 Angle of Attack.** A downward diagonal slash, stab, or strike toward the right side of the defender's head, neck, or torso.

c. **No. 3 Angle of Attack.** A horizontal attack to the left side of the defender's torso in the ribs, side, or hip region.

d. **No. 4 Angle of Attack.** The same as No. 3 angle, but to the right side.

e. **No. 5 Angle of Attack.** A jabbing, lunging, or punching attack directed straight toward the defender's front.

f. **No. 6 Angle of Attack.** An attack directed straight down upon the defender.

g. **No. 7 Angle of Attack.** An upward diagonal attack toward the defender's lower-left side.

h. **No. 8 Angle of Attack.** An upward diagonal attack toward the defender's lower-right side.

i. **No. 9 Angle of Attack.** An attack directed straight up—for example, to the defender's groin.

7-2. RIFLE WITH FIXED BAYONET

The principles used in fighting with the rifle and fixed bayonet are the same as when knife fighting. Use the same angles of attack and similar body movements. The principles of timing and distance remain paramount; the main difference is the extended distance provided by the length of the weapon. It is imperative that the soldier fighting with rifle and fixed bayonet use the movement of his entire body behind all of his fighting techniques—not just upper-body strength. Unit trainers should be especially conscious of stressing full body mass in motion for power and correcting all deficiencies during training. Whether the enemy is armed or unarmed, a soldier fighting with rifle and fixed bayonet must develop the mental attitude that he will survive the fight. He must continuously evaluate each moment in a fight to determine his advantages or options, as well as the enemy's. He should base his defenses on keeping his body moving and off the line of any attacks from his opponent. The soldier seeks openings in the enemy's defenses and starts his own attacks, using all available body weapons and angles of attack. The angles of attack with rifle and fixed bayonet are shown in Figures 7-2 through 7-8.

Figure 7-2. No. 1 angle of attack with rifle and fixed bayonet.

Figure 7-3. No. 2 angle of attack with rifle and fixed bayonet.

Figure 7-4. No. 3 angle of attack with rifle and fixed bayonet.

Figure 7-5. No. 4 angle of attack with rifle and fixed bayonet.

Figure 7-6. Low No. 5 angle of attack with rifle and fixed bayonet.

Figure 7-7. High No. 5 angle of attack with rifle and fixed bayonet.

Figure 7-8. No. 6 angle of attack with rifle and fixed bayonet.

a. **Fighting Techniques**. New weapons, improved equipment, and new tactics are always being introduced; however, firepower alone will not always drive a determined enemy from his position. He will often remain in defensive emplacements until driven out by close combat. The role of the soldier, particularly in the final phase of the assault, remains relatively unchanged: His mission is to close with and kill, disable, or capture the enemy. This mission remains the ultimate goal of all individual training. The rifle with fixed bayonet is one of the final means of defeating an opponent in an assault.

(1) During infiltration missions at night or when secrecy must be maintained, the bayonet is an excellent silent weapon.

(2) When close-in fighting determines the use of small-arms fire or grenades to be impractical, or when the situation does not permit the loading or reloading of the rifle, the bayonet is still the weapon available to the soldier.

(3) The bayonet serves as a secondary weapon should the rifle develop a stoppage.

(4) In hand-to-hand encounters, the detached bayonet may be used as a handheld weapon.

(5) The bayonet has many nonfighting uses, such as to probe for mines, to cut vegetation, and to use for other tasks where a pointed or cutting tool is needed.

b. **Development**. To become a successful rifle-bayonet fighter, a soldier must be physically fit and mentally alert. A well-rounded physical training program will increase his chances of survival in a bayonet encounter. Mental alertness entails being able to quickly detect and meet an opponent's attack from any direction. Aggressiveness, accuracy, balance, and speed are essential in training as well as in combat situations. These traits lead to confidence, coordination, strength, and endurance, which characterize the rifle-bayonet fighter. Differences in individual body physique may require slight changes from the described rifle-bayonet techniques. These variations will be allowed if the individual's attack is effective.

c. **Principles**. The bayonet is an effective weapon to be used aggressively; hesitation may mean sudden death. The soldier must attack in a relentless assault until his opponent is disabled or captured. He should be alert to take advantage of any opening. If the opponent fails to present an opening, the bayonet fighter must make one by parrying his opponent's weapon and driving his blade or rifle butt into the opponent with force.

(1) The attack should be made to a vulnerable part of the body: face, throat, chest, abdomen, or groin.

(2) In both training and combat, the rifle-bayonet fighter displays spirit by sounding off with a low and aggressive growl. This instills a feeling of confidence in his ability to close with and disable or capture the enemy.

(3) The instinctive rifle-bayonet fighting system is designed to capitalize on the natural agility and combative movements of the soldier. It must be emphasized that precise learned movements will NOT be stressed during training.

d. **Positions**. The soldier holds the rifle firmly but not rigidly. He relaxes all muscles not used in a specific position; tense muscles cause fatigue and may slow him down. After proper training and thorough practice, the soldier instinctively assumes the basic positions. All positions and movements described in this manual are for right-handed men. A left-handed man, or a man who desires to learn left-handed techniques, must use the opposite hand and foot for each phase of the movement described. All positions and movements can be executed with or without the magazine and with or without the sling attached.

(1) *Attack Position*. This is the basic starting position (A and B, Figure 7-9) from which all attack movements originate. It generally parallels a boxer's stance. The soldier assumes this position when running or hurdling obstacles. The instructor explains and demonstrates each move.

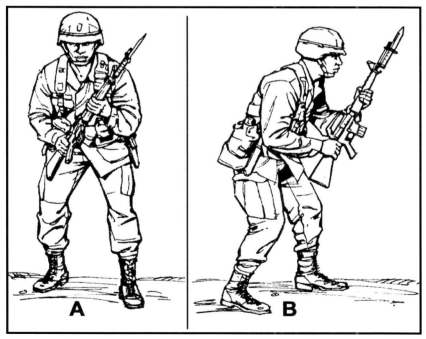

Figure 7-9. Attack position.

(a) Take a step forward and to the side with your left foot so that your feet are a comfortable distance apart.

(b) Hold your body erect or bend slightly forward at the waist. Flex your knees and balance your body weight on the balls of your feet. Your right forearm is roughly parallel to the ground. Hold the left arm high, generally in front of the left shoulder. Maintain eye-to-eye contact with your opponent, watching his weapon and body through peripheral vision.

(c) Hold your rifle diagonally across your body at a sufficient distance from the body to add balance and protect you from enemy blows. Grasp the weapon in your left hand just below the upper sling swivel, and place the right hand at the small of the stock. Keep the sling facing outward and the cutting edge of the bayonet toward your opponent. The command is, ATTACK POSITION, MOVE. The instructor gives the command, and the soldiers perform the movement.

(2) *Relaxed Position.* The relaxed position (Figure 7-10) gives the soldier a chance to rest during training. It also allows him to direct his attention toward the instructor as he discusses and demonstrates the positions and movements. To assume the relaxed position from the attack position, straighten the waist and knees and lower the rifle across the front of your body by extending the arms downward. The command is, RELAX. The instructor gives the command, and the soldiers perform the movement.

Figure 7-10. Relaxed position.

e. *Movements.* The soldier will instinctively strike at openings and become aggressive in his attack once he has learned to relax and has developed instinctive reflexes. His movements do not have to be executed in any prescribed order. He will achieve balance in his movements, be ready to strike in any direction, and keep striking until he has disabled his opponent. There are two basic movements used throughout bayonet instruction: the whirl and the crossover. These movements develop instant reaction to commands and afford the instructor maximum control of the training formation while on the training field.

(1) **Whirl Movement.** The whirl (Figure 7-11, Steps 1, 2, and 3), properly executed, allows the rifle-bayonet fighter to meet a challenge from an opponent attacking him from the rear. At the completion of a whirl, the rifle remains in the attack position. The instructor explains and demonstrates how to spin your body around by pivoting on the ball of the leading foot in the direction of the leading foot, thus facing completely about. The command is, WHIRL. The instructor gives the command, and the soldiers perform the movement.

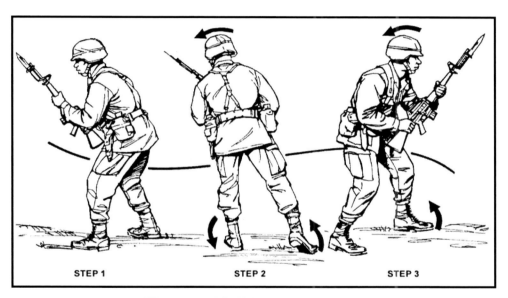

Figure 7-11. Whirl movement.

(2) **Crossover Movement.** While performing certain movements in rifle-bayonet training, two ranks will be moving toward each other. When the soldiers in ranks come too close to each other to safely execute additional movements, the crossover is used to separate the ranks a safe distance apart. The instructor explains and demonstrates how to move straight forward and pass your opponent so that your right shoulder passes his right shoulder, continue moving forward about six steps, halt, and without command, execute the whirl. Remain in the attack position and wait for further commands. The command is, CROSSOVER. The instructor gives the command, and the soldiers perform the movement.

Note: Left-handed personnel cross left shoulder to left shoulder.

(3) **Attack Movements.** There are four attack movements designed to disable or capture the opponent: thrust, butt stroke, slash, and smash. Each of these movements may

be used for the initial attack or as a follow-up should the initial movement fail to find its mark. The soldiers learn these movements separately. They will learn to execute these movements in a swift and continuous series during subsequent training. During all training, the emphasis will be on conducting natural, balanced movements to effectively damage the target. Precise, learned movements will not be stressed.

(a) *Thrust*. The objective is to disable or capture an opponent by thrusting the bayonet blade into a vulnerable part of his body. The thrust is especially effective in areas where movement is restricted—for example, trenches, wooded areas, or built-up areas. It is also effective when an opponent is lying on the ground or in a fighting position. The instructor explains and demonstrates how to lunge forward on your leading foot without losing your balance (Figure 7-12, Step 1) and, at the same time, drive the bayonet with great force into any unguarded part of your opponent's body.

- To accomplish this, grasp the rifle firmly with both hands and pull the stock in close to the right hip; partially extend the left arm, guiding the point of the bayonet in the general direction of the opponent's body (Figure 7-12, Step 2).
- Quickly complete the extension of the arms and body as the leading foot strikes the ground so that the bayonet penetrates the target (Figure 7-12, Step 3).
- To withdraw the bayonet, keep your feet in place, shift your body weight to the rear, and pull rearward along the same line of penetration (Figure 7-12, Step 4).
- Next, assume the attack position in preparation to continue the assault (Figure 7-12, Step 5). This movement is taught by the numbers in three phases:

  1. **THRUST AND HOLD, MOVE.**
  2. **WITHDRAW AND HOLD, MOVE.**
  3. **ATTACK POSITION, MOVE.**

- At combat speed, the command is, THRUST SERIES, MOVE. Training emphasis will be placed on movement at combat speed. The instructor gives the commands, and the soldiers perform the movements.

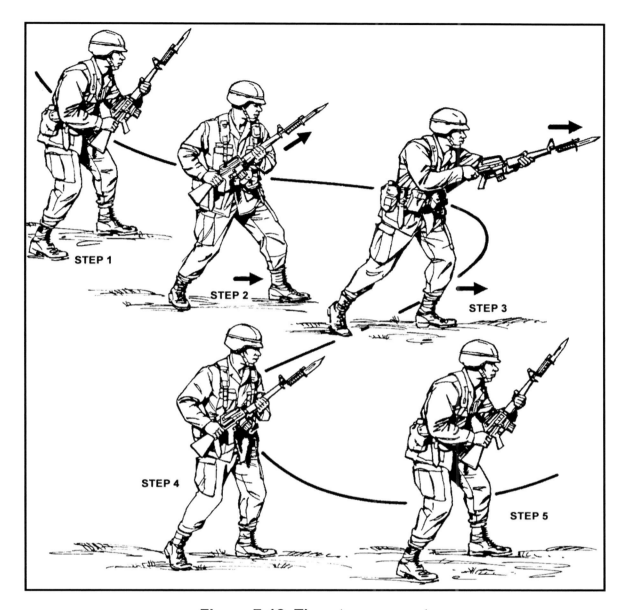

Figure 7-12. Thrust movement.

(b) *Butt Stroke.* The objective is to disable or capture an opponent by delivering a forceful blow to his body with the rifle butt (Figure 7-13, Steps 1, 2, 3, and 4, and Figure 7-14, Steps 1, 2, 3, and 4). The aim of the butt stroke may be the opponent's weapon or a vulnerable portion of his body. The butt stroke may be vertical, horizontal, or somewhere between the two planes. The instructor explains and demonstrates how to step forward with your trailing foot and, at the same time using your left hand as a pivot, swing the rifle in an arc and drive the rifle butt into your opponent. To recover, bring your trailing foot forward and assume the attack position. The movement is taught by the numbers in two phases:

    1. BUTT STROKE TO THE (head, groin, kidney) **AND HOLD, MOVE.**
    2. ATTACK POSITION, MOVE.

At combat speed, the command is, BUTT STROKE TO THE (head, groin, kidney) SERIES, MOVE. Training emphasis will be placed on movement at combat speed. The instructor gives the commands, and the soldiers perform the movement.

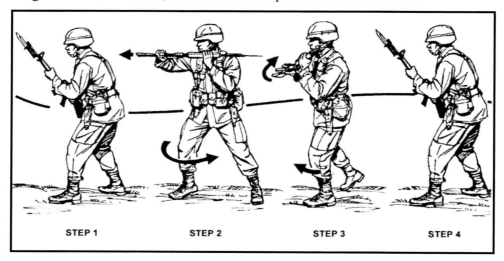

Figure 7-13. Butt stroke to the head.

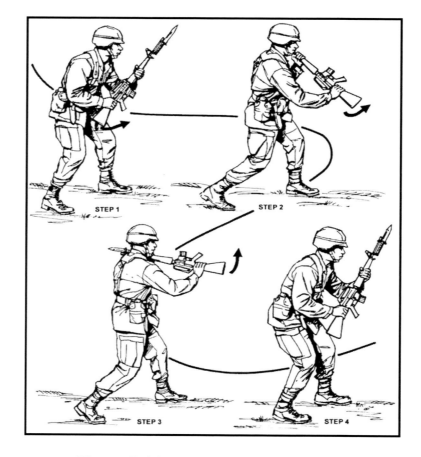

Figure 7-14. Butt stroke to the groin.

(c) *Slash*. The objective is to disable or capture the opponent by cutting him with the blade of the bayonet. The instructor explains and demonstrates how to step forward with your lead foot (Figure 7-15, Step 1).

- At the same time, extend your left arm and swing the knife edge of your bayonet forward and down in a slashing arc (Figure 7-15, Steps 2 and 3).
- To recover, bring your trailing foot forward and assume the attack position (Figure 5-15, Step 4). This movement is taught by the number in two phases:
  1. **SLASH AND HOLD, MOVE.**
  2. **ATTACK POSITION, MOVE.**
- At combat speed, the command is, SLASH SERIES, MOVE. Training emphasis will be placed on movement at combat speed. The instructor gives the commands, and the soldiers perform the movements.

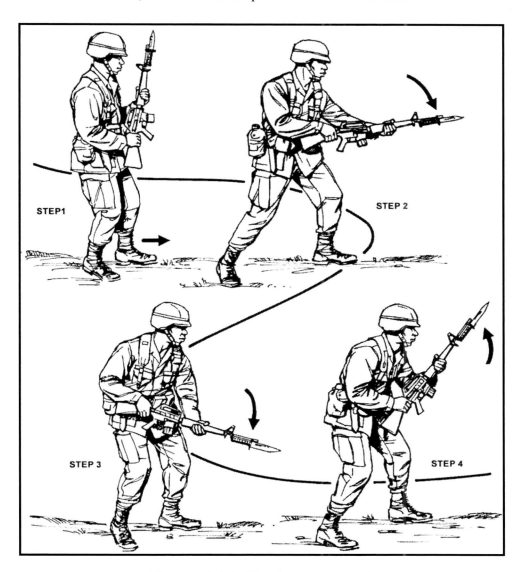

Figure 7-15. Slash movement.

(d) *Smash*. The objective is to disable or capture an opponent by smashing the rifle butt into a vulnerable part of his body. The smash is often used as a follow-up to a butt stroke and is also effective in wooded areas and trenches when movement is restricted. The instructor explains and demonstrates how to push the butt of the rifle upward until horizontal (Figure 7-16, Step 1) and above the left shoulder with the bayonet pointing to the rear, sling up (Figure 7-16, Step 2). The weapon is almost horizontal to the ground at this time.

- Step forward with the trailing foot, as in the butt stroke, and forcefully extend both arms, slamming the rifle butt into the opponent (Figure 7-16, Step 3).
- To recover, bring your trailing foot forward (Figure 7-16, Step 4) and assume the attack position (Figure 7-16, Step 5). This movement is taught by the numbers in two phases:
  1. **SMASH AND HOLD, MOVE.**
  2. **ATTACK POSITION, MOVE.**
- At combat speed, the command is, SMASH SERIES, MOVE. Training emphasis will be placed on movement at combat speed. The instructor gives the commands, and the soldiers perform the movements.

Figure 7-16. Smash movement.

(4) *Defensive Movements*. At times, the soldier may lose the initiative and be forced to defend himself. He may also meet an opponent who does not present a vulnerable area to attack. Therefore, he must make an opening by initiating a parry or block movement, then follow up with a vicious attack. The follow-up attack is immediate and violent.

> **CAUTION**
> To minimize weapon damage while using blocks and parries, limit weapon-to-weapon contact to half speed during training.

(a) *Parry Movement*. The objective is to counter a thrust, throw the opponent off balance, and hit a vulnerable area of his body. Timing, speed, and judgment are essential factors in these movements. The instructor explains and demonstrates how to—

- Parry right. If your opponent carries his weapon on his left hip (left-handed), you will parry it to your right. In execution, step forward with your leading foot (Figure 7-17, Step 1), strike the opponent's rifle (Figure 7-17, Step 2), deflecting it to your right (Figure 7-17, Step 3), and follow up with a thrust, slash, or butt stroke.

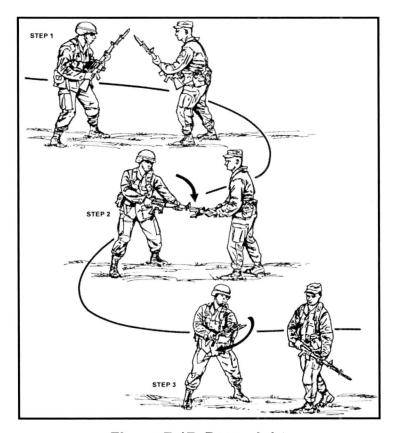

Figure 7-17. Parry right.

- Parry left. If your opponent carries his weapon on his right hip (right-handed), you will parry it to your left. In execution, step forward with your leading foot (Figure 7-18, Step 1), strike the opponent's rifle (Figure 7-18, Step 2), deflecting it to your left (Figure 7-18, Step 3), and follow up with a thrust, slash, or butt stroke. A supplementary parry left is the follow-up attack (Figure 7-19, Steps 1, 2, 3, 4, and 5).

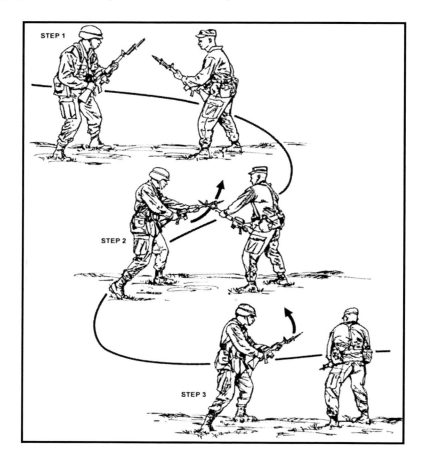

Figure 7-18. Parry left.

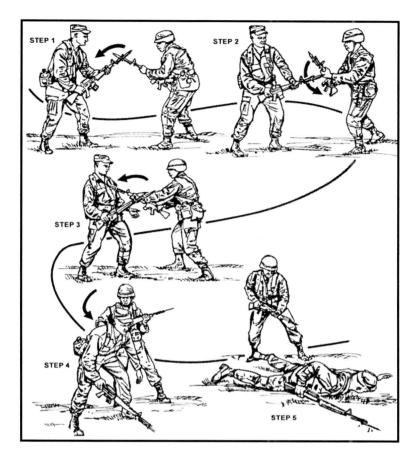

Figure 7-19. Parry left, slash, with follow-up butt stroke to kidney region.

- Recovery. Immediately return to the attack position after completing each parry and follow-up attack. The movement is taught by the numbers in three phases:
  1. **PARRY RIGHT (OR LEFT), MOVE.**
  2. **THRUST, MOVE.**
  3. **ATTACK POSITION, MOVE.**
- At combat speed, the command is, PARRY RIGHT (LEFT) or PARRY (RIGHT OR LEFT) WITH FOLLOW-UP ATTACK. The instructor gives the commands, and the soldiers perform the movements.

(b) *Block.* When surprised by an opponent, the block is used to cut off the path of his attack by making weapon-to-weapon contact. A block must always be followed immediately with a vicious attack. The instructor explains and demonstrates how to extend your arms using the center part of your rifle as the strike area, and cut off the opponent's attack by making weapon-to-weapon contact. Strike the opponent's weapon with enough power to throw him off balance. Blocks are taught by the numbers in two phases:
  1. **HIGH (LOW) or (SIDE) BLOCK.**
  2. **ATTACK POSITION, MOVE.**

- High block (Figure 7-20, Steps 1, 2, and 3). Extend your arms upward and forward at a 45-degree angle. This action deflects an opponent's slash movement by causing his bayonet or upper part of his rifle to strike against the center part of your rifle.

Figure 7-20. High block against slash.

- Low block (Figure 7-21, Steps 1, 2, and 3). Extend your arms downward and forward about 15 degrees from your body. This action deflects an opponent's butt stroke aimed at the groin by causing the lower part of his rifle stock to strike against the center part of your rifle.

Figure 7-21. Low block against butt stroke to groin.

- Side block (Figure 7-22, Steps 1 and 2). Extend your arms with the left hand high and right hand low, thus holding the rifle vertical. This block is designed to stop a butt stroke aimed at your upper body or head. Push the rifle to your left to cause the butt of the opponent's rifle to strike the center portion of your rifle.
- Recovery. Counterattack each block with a thrust, butt stroke, smash, or slash.
- At combat speed, the command is the same. The instructor gives the commands, and the soldiers perform the movement.

Figure 7-22. Side block against butt stroke.

(5) *Modified Movements*. Two attack movements have been modified to allow the rifle-bayonet fighter to slash or thrust an opponent without removing his hand from the pistol grip of the M16 rifle should the situation dictate.

(a) The modified thrust (Figure 7-23, Steps 1 and 2) is identical to the thrust with the exception of the right hand grasping the pistol grip.

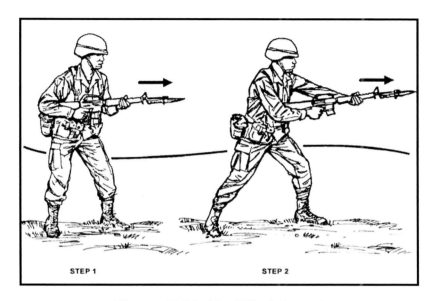

Figure 7-23. Modified thrust.

(b) The modified slash (Figure 7-24, Steps 1, 2, 3, and 4) is identical to the slash with the exception of the right hand grasping the pistol grip.

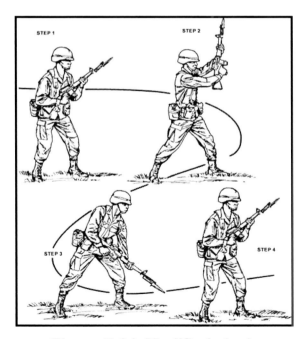

Figure 7-24. Modified slash.

(6) *Follow-up Movements*. Follow-up movements are attack movements that naturally follow from the completed position of the previous movement. If the initial thrust, butt stroke, smash, or slash fails to make contact with the opponent's body, the soldier should instinctively follow up with additional movements until he has disabled or captured the opponent. It is important to follow-up the initial attack with another aggressive action so the initiative is not lost. The instructor explains and demonstrates how instinct should govern your selection of a specific follow-up movement. For example—

- **PARRY LEFT, BUTT STROKE TO THE HEAD, SMASH, SLASH, ATTACK POSITION**.
- **PARRY LEFT, SLASH, BUTT STROKE TO THE KIDNEY, ATTACK POSITION**.
- **PARRY RIGHT, THRUST, BUTT STROKE TO THE GROIN, SLASH, ATTACK POSITION**.

Two examples of commands using follow-up movements are:
- **PARRY LEFT** (soldier executes), **THRUST** (soldier executes), **BUTT STROKE TO THE HEAD** (soldier executes), **SMASH** (soldier executes), **SLASH** (soldier executes), **ATTACK POSITION** (soldier assumes the attack position).
- **THRUST** (soldier executes), **THRUST** (soldier executes), **THRUST** (soldier executes), **BUTT STROKE TO THE GROIN** (soldier executes), **SLASH** (soldier executes), **ATTACK POSITION** (soldier assumes the attack position).

All training will stress damage to the target and violent action, using natural movements as opposed to precise, stereotyped movements. Instinctive, aggressive action and balance are the keys to offense with the rifle and bayonet.

Note: For training purposes, the instructor may and should mix up the series of movements.

7-3. BAYONET/KNIFE

As the bayonet is an integral part of the combat soldier's equipment, it is readily available for use as a multipurpose weapon. The bayonet produces a terrifying mental effect on the enemy when in the hands of a well-trained and confident soldier. The soldier skilled in the use of the knife also increases his ability to defend against larger opponents and multiple attackers. Both these skills increase his chances of surviving and accomplishing the mission. (Although the following paragraphs say "knife," the information also applies to bayonets.)

a. **Grips**. The best way to hold the knife is either with the straight grip or the reverse grip.

(1) *Straight Grip*. Grip the knife in the strong hand by forming a "vee" and by allowing the knife to fit naturally, as in gripping for a handshake. The handle should lay diagonally across the palm. Point the blade toward the enemy, usually with the cutting

edge down. The cutting edge can also be held vertically or horizontally to the ground. Use the straight grip when thrusting and slashing.

(2) **Reverse Grip**. Grip the knife with the blade held parallel with the forearm, cutting edge facing outward. This grip conceals the knife from the enemy's view. The reverse grip also affords the most power for lethal insertion. Use this grip for slashing, stabbing, and tearing.

b. **Stances**. The primary stances are the knife fighter's stance and the modified stance.

(1) **Knife Fighter's Stance**. In this stance, the fighter stands with his feet about shoulder-width apart, dominant foot toward the rear. About 70 percent of his weight is on the front foot and 30 percent on the rear foot. He stands on the balls of both feet and holds the knife with the straight grip. The other hand is held close to his body where it is ready to use, but protected (Figure 7-25).

Figure 7-25. Knife fighter's stance.

(2) *Modified Stance*. The difference in the modified stance is the knife is held close to the body with the other hand held close over the knife hand to help conceal it (Figure 7-26).

Figure 7-26. Modified stance.

c. **Range.** The two primary ranges in knife fighting are long range and medium range. In long-range knife fighting, attacks consist of figure-eight slashes along the No. 1, No. 2, No. 7, and No. 8 angles of attack; horizontal slashes along the No. 3 and No. 4 angles of attack; and lunging thrusts to vital areas on the No. 5 angle of attack. Usually, the straight grip is used. In medium-range knife fighting, the reverse grip provides greater power. It is used to thrust, slash, and tear along all angles of attack.

7-4.   KNIFE-AGAINST-KNIFE SEQUENCE
The knife fighter must learn to use all available weapons of his body and not limit himself to the knife. The free hand can be used to trap the enemy's hands to create openings in his defense. The enemy's attention will be focused on the weapon; therefore, low kicks and knee strikes will seemingly come from nowhere. The knife fighter's priority of targets are the eyes, throat, abdominal region, and extended limbs. The following knife attack sequences can be used in training to help develop soldiers' knowledge of movements, principles, and techniques in knife fighting.

a. **Nos. 1 and 4 Angles**. Two opponents assume the knife fighter's stance (Figure 7-27, Step 1). The attacker starts with a diagonal slash along the No. 1 angle of attack to the throat (Figure 7-27, Step 2). He then follows through with a slash and continues with a horizontal slash back across the abdomen along the No. 4 angle of attack (Figure 7-27, Step 3).He finishes the attack by using his entire body mass behind a lunging stab into the opponent's solar plexus (Figure 7-27, Step 4).

Figure 7-27. Nos. 1 and 4 angles.

b. **Nos. 5, 3, and 2 Angles**. In this sequence, one opponent (attacker) starts an attack with a lunge along the No. 5 angle of attack. At the same time, the other opponent (defender) on the left moves his body off the line of attack, parries the attacking arm, and slices the biceps of his opponent (Figure 7-28, Step 1). The defender slashes back across the groin along the No. 3 angle of attack (Figure 7-28, Step 2). He finishes the attacker by continuing with an upward stroke into the armpit or throat along the No. 2 angle of attack (Figure 7-28, Step 3). Throughout this sequence, the attacker's weapon hand is controlled with the defenders left hand as he attacks with his own knife hand.

Figure 7-28. Nos. 5, 3, and 2 angles.

c. **Low No. 5 Angle**. In the next sequence, the attacker on the right lunges to the stomach along a low No. 5 angle of attack. The defender on the left moves his body off the line of attack while parrying and slashing the wrist of the attacking knife hand as he redirects the arm (Figure 7-29, Step 1). After he slashes the wrist of his attacker, the defender continues to move around the outside and stabs the attacker's armpit (Figure 7-29, Step 2). He retracts his knife from the armpit, continues his movement around the attacker, and slices his hamstring (Figure 7-29, Step 3).

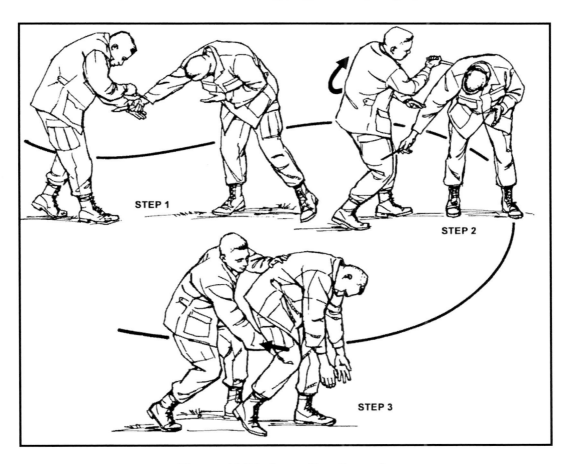

Figure 7-29. Low No. 5 angle.

d. **Optional Low No. 5 Angle**. The attacker on the right lunges to the stomach of his opponent (the defender) along the low No. 5 angle of attack. The defender moves his body off the line of attack of the knife. Then he turns and, at the same time, delivers a slash to the attacker's throat along the No. 1 angle of attack (Figure 7-30, Step 1). he defender immediately follows with another slash to the opposite side of the attacker's throat along the No. 2 angle of attack (Figure 7-30, Step 2). The attacker is finished as the opponent on the left (defender) continues to slice across the abdomen with a stroke along the No. 3 angle (Figure 7-30, Step 3).

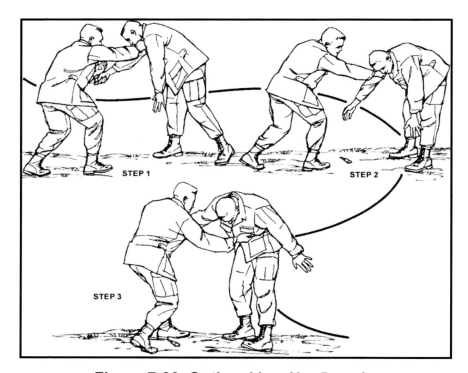

Figure 7-30. Optional low No. 5 angle.

7-5. ADVANCED WEAPONS TECHNIQUES AND TRAINING

For advanced training in weapons techniques, training partners should have the same skill level. Attackers can execute attacks along multiple angles of attack in combinations. The attacker must attack with a speed that offers the defender a challenge, but does not overwhelm him. It should not be a contest to see who can win, but a training exercise for both individuals.

a. Continued training in weapons techniques will lead to the partners' ability to engage in free-response fighting or sparring—that is, the individuals become adept enough to understand the principles of weapons attacks, defense, and movements so they can respond freely when attacking or defending from any angle.

b. Instructors must closely monitor training partners to ensure that the speed and control of the individuals does not become dangerous during advanced training practice. Proper eye protection and padding should be used, when applicable. The instructor should stress the golden rule in free-response fighting—Do unto others as you would have them do unto you.

Section II. FIELD-EXPEDIENT WEAPONS

To survive, the soldier in combat must be able to deal with any situation that develops. His ability to adapt any nearby object for use as a weapon in a win-or-die situation is limited only by his ingenuity and resourcefulness. Possible weapons, although not discussed herein, include ink pens or pencils; canteens tied to string to be swung; snap links at the end of sections of rope; kevlar helmets; sand, rocks, or liquids thrown into the enemy's eyes; or radio antennas. The following techniques demonstrate a few expedient weapons that are readily available to most soldiers for defense and counterattack against the bayonet and rifle with fixed bayonet.

7-6. ENTRENCHING TOOL

Almost all soldiers carry the entrenching tool. It is a versatile and formidable weapon when used by a soldier with some training. It can be used in its straight position—locked out and fully extended—or with its blade bent in a 90-degree configuration.

a. To use the entrenching tool against a rifle with fixed bayonet, the attacker lunges with a thrust to the stomach of the defender along a low No. 5 angle of attack (Figure 7-31, Step 1).

(1) The defender moves just outside to avoid the lunge and meets the attacker's arm with the blade of the fully extended entrenching tool (Figure 7-31, Step 2).

(2) The defender gashes all the way up the attacker's arm with the force of both body masses coming together. The hand gripping the entrenching tool is given natural protection from the shape of the handle. The defender continues pushing the blade of the entrenching tool up and into the throat of the attacker, driving him backward and downward (Figure 7-31, Step 3).

Figure 7-31. Entrenching tool against rifle with fixed bayonet.

b. An optional use of entrenching tool against a rifle with fixed bayonet is for the attacker to lunge to the stomach of the defender (Figure 7-32, Step 1).

(1) The defender steps to the outside of the line of attack at 45 degrees to avoid the weapon. He then turns his body and strikes downward onto the attacking arm (on the radial nerve) with the blade of the entrenching tool (Figure 7-32, Step 2).

(2) He drops his full body weight down with the strike, and the force causes the attacker to collapse forward. The defender then strikes the point of the entrenching tool into the jugular notch, driving it deeply into the attacker (Figure 7-32, Step 3).

Figure 7-32. Optional use of the entrenching tool against rifle with fixed bayonet.

c.   In the next two sequences, the entrenching tool is used in the bent configuration—that is, the blade is bent 90 degrees to the handle and locked into place.

(1) The attacker tries to stick the bayonet into the chest of the defender (Figure 7-33, Step 1).

(a) When the attack comes, the defender moves his body off the line of attack by stepping to the outside. He allows his weight to shift forward and uses the blade of the entrenching tool to drag along the length of the weapon, scraping the attacker's arm and hand (Figure 7-33, Step 2). The defender's hand is protected by the handle's natural design.

(b) He continues to move forward into the attacker, strikes the point of the blade into the jugular notch, and drives it downward (Figure 7-33, Step 3).

Figure 7-33. Entrenching tool in bent configuration.

(2) The attacker lunges with a fixed bayonet along the No. 5 angle of attack (Figure 7-34, Step 1). The defender then steps to the outside to move off the line of attack and turns; he strikes the point of the blade of the entrenching tool into the side of the attacker's throat (Figure 7-34, Step 2).

Figure 7-34. Optional use of entrenching tool in bent configuration.

7-7. THREE-FOOT STICK

Since a stick can be found almost anywhere, a soldier should know its uses as a field-expedient weapon. The stick is a versatile weapon; its capability ranges from simple prisoner control to lethal combat.

a. Use a stick about 3 feet long and grip it by placing it in the "vee" formed between the thumb and index finger, as in a handshake. It may also be grasped by two hands and used in an unlimited number of techniques. The stick is not held at the end, but at a comfortable distance from the butt end.

b. When striking with the stick, achieve maximum power by using the entire body weight behind each blow. The desired point of contact of the weapon is the last 2 inches at the tip of the stick. The primary targets for striking with the stick are the vital body points in Chapter 4. Effective striking points are usually the wrist, hand, knees, and other bony protuberances. Soft targets include the side of the neck, jugular notch, solar plexus, and various nerve motor points. Attack soft targets by striking or thrusting the tip of the stick into the area. Three basic methods of striking are—

(1) **Thrusting**. Grip the stick with both hands and thrust straight into a target with the full body mass behind it.

(2) **Whipping**. Hold the stick in one hand and whip it in a circular motion; use the whole body mass in motion to generate power.

(3) **Snapping**. Snap the stick in short, shocking blows, again with the body mass behind each strike.

(a) When the attacker thrusts with a knife to the stomach of the defender with a low No. 5 angle of attack, the defender moves off the line of attack to the outside and strikes vigorously downward onto the attacking wrist, hand, or arm (Figure 7-35, page 7-34, Step 1).

(b) The defender then moves forward, thrusts the tip of the stick into the jugular notch of the attacker (Figure 7-35, Step 2), and drives him to the ground with his body weight—not his upper body strength (Figure 7-35, Step 3).

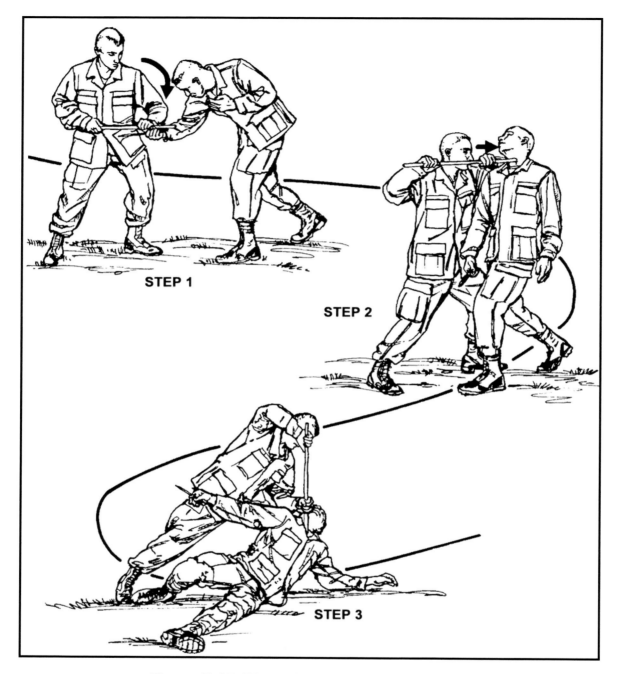

Figure 7-35. Three-foot stick against knife.

c. When using a three-foot stick against a rifle with fixed bayonet, the defender grasps the stick with two hands, one at each end, as the attacker thrusts forward to the chest (Figure 7-36, Step 1).

(1) He steps off the line of attack to the outside and redirects the weapon with the stick (Figure 7-36, Step 2).

(2) He then strikes forward with the forearm into the attacker's throat (Figure 7-36, Step 3). The force of the two body weights coming together is devastating. The attacker's neck is trapped in the notch formed by the stick and the defender's forearm.

(3) Using the free end of the stick as a lever, the defender steps back and uses his body weight to drive the attacker to the ground. The leverage provided by the stick against the neck creates a tremendous choke with the forearm, and the attacker loses control completely (Figure 7-36, Step 4).

Figure 7-36. Three-foot stick against rifle with fixed bayonet.

7-8. SIX-FOOT POLE
Another field-expedient weapon that can mean the difference between life and death for a soldier in an unarmed conflict is a pole about 6 feet long. Examples of poles suitable for use are mop handles, pry bars, track tools, tent poles, and small trees or limbs cut to form a pole. A soldier skilled in the use of a pole as a weapon is a formidable opponent. The size and weight of the pole requires him to move his whole body to use it effectively. Its length gives the soldier an advantage of distance in most unarmed situations. There are two methods usually used in striking with a pole:

    a. **Swinging**. Becoming effective in swinging the pole requires skilled body movement and practice. The greatest power is developed by striking with the last 2 inches of the pole.

    b. **Thrusting**. The pole is thrust straight along its axis with the user's body mass firmly behind it.

    (1) An attacker tries to thrust forward with a fixed bayonet (Figure 7-37, Step 1). The defender moves his body off the line of attack; he holds the tip of the pole so that the attacker runs into it from his own momentum. He then aims for the jugular notch and anchors his body firmly in place so that the full force of the attack is felt at the attacker's throat (Figure 7-37, Step 2).

    (2) The defender then shifts his entire body weight forward over his lead foot and drives the attacker off his feet (Figure 7-37, Step 3).

Note: During high stress, small targets, such as the throat, may be difficult to hit. Good, large targets include the solar plexus and hip/thigh joint.

Figure 7-37. Thrusting with 6-foot pole.

CHAPTER 8
STANDING DEFENSE

A soldier cannot count on starting every encounter in a superior position. To survive, he must have simple techniques that will bring him back into his fight plan.

Section I. UNARMED OPPONENT

Most grasping type attacks will leave the enemy in striking range. Therefore, elaborate defenses are not necessary. You should simply attack with strikes and force the enemy to either close with you, or when he attempts to respond with strikes, take the opportunity to close or escape yourself. The techniques in this section are directed at escaping from positions that are more difficult.

8-1. DEFENSE AGAINST CHOKES

a. **Standing Rear Naked** (Figure 8-1, continued on page 8-2). At the moment you feel the enemy's arm around your neck, your hands should immediately grasp it to keep him from tightening the choke, and you should hang your weight on his arm to feel where his weight is. If he is close to your back, simply lean forward at the waist and, using your hips to lift, throw him straight over your back.

Figure 8-1. Defense against the standing rear naked choke.

Figure 8-1. Defense against the standing rear naked choke (continued).

Figure 8-1. Defense against the standing rear naked choke (continued).

b. **Standing Rear Naked Pulling Back** (Figure 8-2, continued on page 8-3). If, when you hang your weight on the enemy's arm, you feel that he is pulling you back over one of his legs, you should reach back with your leg and wrap it around the outside of the enemy's leg on the same side as the choking arm. As he tires from holding you up, use your leg as a guide and work your way around to the position shown. Your leg must be behind his, and you must be leaning forward, controlling his arm. Twisting your body, throw him to the ground.

Figure 8-2. Defense against the standing rear naked choke leaning back.

Figure 8-2. Defense against the standing rear naked choke leaning back (continued).

Figure 8-2. Defense against the standing rear naked choke leaning back (continued).

c. **One-Hand Neck Press Against the Wall** (Figure 8-3). If the enemy pins you against the wall with one hand, strike his arm with the palm of your hand on the side where his thumb is pushing toward his fingers. This will make his arm slide off of your neck. Follow through with your strike and when your arm is in position, strike with a backward elbow strike to the head.

Figure 8-3. Defense against one-hand neck press against a wall.

Figure 8-3. Defense against one-hand neck press against a wall (continued).

d. **Two-Hand Neck Press While Pinned Against the Wall** (Figure 8-4). If the enemy uses both hands against your neck to press you into the wall, grasp under his elbows with both hands. Step out to either side and throw him against the wall. Finish with a knee strike.

Figure 8-4. Defense against the two-hand neck press against a wall.

Figure 8-4. Defense against the two-hand neck press against a wall (continued).

Figure 8-4. Defense against the two-hand neck press against a wall (continued).

8-2. DEFENSE AGAINST BEAR HUGS

a. **Front Bear Hug Over Your Arms** (Figure 8-5, continued on page 8-8). If the enemy attempts to grasp you in a bear hug from the front over your arms, move your hips back and use your arms as a brace between his hips and yours. Your hands should be on his hip bones, and your elbows should be braced against your hips. Keeping one arm as a brace, step to the opposite side to achieve the clinch. Finish with a takedown.

Figure 8-5. Defense against the front bear hug over your arms.

Figure 8-5. Defense against the front bear hug over your arms (continued).

b. **Front Bear Hug Under Your Arms** (Figure 8-6). If the enemy attempts to grasp you under your arms, step back into a strong base and use both hands to push his chin upwards to break his grasp. Finish with a knee strike. If he is exceptionally strong, push upwards against his nose.

Figure 8-6. Defense against the front bear hug under your arms.

Figure 8-6. Defense against the front bear hug under your arms (continued).

c. **Bear Hug From the Rear, Over the Arms** (Figure 8-7, continued on page 8-10). When the enemy attempts to grab you from behind over your arms, drop down into a strong stance and bring your arms up to prevent him from controlling them. Step to the outside and then around his hip so that your legs are behind him. At this point you may attack his groin, or you may lift him with your hips and throw him.

Figure 8-7. Defense against the bear hug from the rear, over the arms.

Figure 8-7. Defense against the bear hug from the rear, over the arms (continued).

d. **Bear Hug from the Rear Under Your Arms** (Figure 8-8, continued on pages 8-12 and 8-13). When the enemy grasps you from the rear under your arms, he will probably try to lift you for a throw. If he does so, wrap your leg around his so that you are harder to maneuver for the throw. When he sets you down, or if he did not lift you in the first place, lean your weight forward and place your hands on the ground. Move to one side until one of his legs is between yours. Push backward slightly and reach one hand back to grasp his heel. When you have a good grip, reach back with the other hand. Pull forward with your hands, and when he falls, break his knee by sitting on it as you pull on his leg.

Figure 8-8. Defense against the bear hug from the rear, under the arms.

Figure 8-8. Defense against the bear hug from the rear, under the arms (continued).

Figure 8-8. Defense against the bear hug from the rear, under the arms (continued).

Figure 8-8. Defense against the bear hug from the rear, under the arms (continued).

CAUTION
Care must be taken when practicing this technique to avoid accidental injury.

Section II. ARMED OPPONENT

A knife (or bayonet), properly employed, is a deadly weapon; however, using defensive techniques, such as maintaining separation, will greatly enhance the soldier's ability to fight and win.

8-3. DEFENSE AGAINST AN ARMED OPPONENT

An unarmed defender is always at a distinct disadvantage when facing an armed opponent. It is imperative, therefore, that the unarmed defender understands and uses the following principles to survive.

a. **Separation**. Maintain a separation of at least 10 feet plus the length of the weapon from the attacker. This distance gives the defender time to react to any attempt by the attacker to close the gap and be upon the defender. The defender should also try to place stationary objects between himself and the attacker.

b. **Unarmed Defense**. Unarmed defense against an armed opponent should be a last resort. If it is necessary, the defender's course of action includes:

(1) *Move the body out of the line of attack of the weapon.* Step off the line of attack or redirect the attack of the weapon so that it clears the body.

(2) *Control the weapon.* Maintain control of the attacking arm by securing the weapon, hand, wrist, elbow, or arm by using joint locks, if possible.

(3) *Stun the attacker with an effective counterattack.* Counterattack should be swift and devastating. Take the vigor out of the attacker with a low, unexpected kick, or break a locked joint of the attacking arm. Strikes to motor nerve centers are effective stuns, as are skin tearing, eye gouging, and attacking of the throat. The defender can also take away the attacker's balance.

(4) *Ground the attacker.* Take the attacker to the ground where the defender can continue to disarm or further disable him.

(5) *Disarm the attacker.* Break the attacker's locked joints. Use leverage or induce pain to disarm the attacker and finish him or to maintain physical control.

c. **Precaution**. Do not focus full attention on the weapon because the attacker has other body weapons to use. There may even be other attackers that you have not seen.

d. **Expedient Aids**. Anything available can become an expedient aid to defend against an armed attack. The Kevlar helmet can be used as a shield; similarly, the LCE and shirt jacket can be used to protect the defender against a weapon. The defender can also throw dirt in the attacker's eyes as a distraction.

8-4.   DEFENSE AGAINST A KNIFE

When an unarmed soldier is faced with an enemy armed with a knife, he must be mentally prepared to be cut. The likelihood of being cut severely is less if the fighter is well trained in knife defense and if the principles of weapon defense are followed. A slash wound is not usually lethal or shock inducing; however, a stab wound risks injury to vital organs, arteries, and veins and may also cause instant shock or unconsciousness.

a. **Types of Knife Attacks**. The first line of defense against an opponent armed with a knife is to avoid close contact. The different types of knife attacks are:

(1) *Thrust.* The thrust is the most common and most dangerous type of knife attack. It is a strike directed straight into the target by jabbing or lunging.

(2) *Slash.* The slash is a sweeping surface cut or circular slash. The wound is usually a long cut, varying from a slight surface cut to a deep gash.

(3) *Tear.* The tear is a cut made by dragging the tip of the blade across the body to create a ripping-type cut.

(4) *Hack.* The hack is delivered by using the knife to block or chop with.

(5) *Butt.* The butt is a strike with the knife handle.

b. **Knife Defense Drills**. Knife defense drills are used to familiarize soldiers with defense movement techniques for various angles of attack. For training, the soldiers should be paired off; one partner is named as the attacker and one is the defender. It is important that the attacker make his attack realistic in terms of distance and angling during training. His strikes must be accurate in hitting the defender at the intended target if the defender does not defend himself or move off the line of attack. For safety, the attacks are delivered first at one-quarter and one-half speed, and then at three-quarter speed as the defender becomes more skilled. Variations can be added by changing grips, stances, and attacks.

(1) *No. 1 Angle of Defense—Check and Lift* (Figure 8-9). The attacker delivers a slash along the No. 1 angle of attack. The defender meets and checks the movement with his left forearm bone, striking the inside forearm of the attacker (Step 1). The defender's

right hand immediately follows behind the strike to lift, redirect, and take control of the attacker's knife arm (Step 2). The defender brings the attacking arm around to his right side where he can use an arm bar, wrist lock, and so forth, to disarm the attacker (Step 3). He will have better control by keeping the knife hand as close to his body as possible (Step 4).

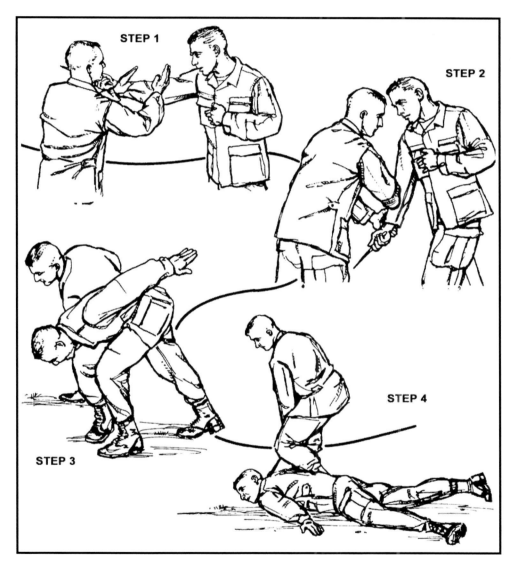

Figure 8-9. No. 1 angle of defense—check and lift.

(2) *No. 2 Angle of Defense—Check and Ride* (Figure 8-10). The attacker slashes with a No. 2 angle of attack. The defender meets the attacking arm with a strike from both forearms against the outside forearm, his bone against the attacker's muscle tissue (Step 1). The strike checks the forward momentum of the attacking arm. The defender's right hand is then used to ride the attacking arm clear of his body (Step 2). He redirects the attacker's energy with strength starting from the right elbow (Step 3).

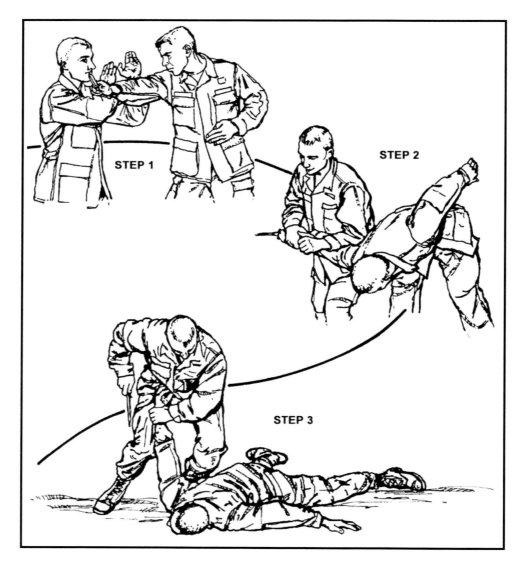

Figure 8-10. No. 2 angle of defense—check and ride.

(3) *No. 3 Angle of Defense—Check and Lift* (Figure 8-11). The attacker delivers a horizontal slash to the defender's ribs, kidneys, or hip on the left side (Step 1). The defender meets and checks the attacking arm on the left side of his body with a downward circular motion across the front of his own body. At the same time, he moves his body off the line of attack. He should meet the attacker's forearm with a strike forceful enough to check its momentum (Step 2). The defender then rides the energy of the attacking arm by wiping downward along the outside of his own left forearm with his right hand. He then redirects the knife hand around to his right side where he can control or disarm the weapon (Step 3).

Figure 8-11. No. 3 angle of defense—check and lift.

(4) *No. 4 Angle of Defense—Check* (Figure 8-12). The attacker slashes the defender with a backhand slashing motion to the right side at the ribs, kidneys, or hips. The defender moves his right arm in a downward circular motion and strikes the attacking arm on the outside of the body (Step 1). At the same time, he moves off the line of attack (Step 2). The strike must be forceful enough to check the attack. The left arm is held in a higher guard position to protect from a redirected attack or to assist in checking (Step 3). The defender moves his body to a position where he can choose a proper disarming maneuver (Step 4).

Figure 8-12. No. 4 angle of defense—check.

(5) *Low No. 5 Angle of Defense--Parry* (Figure 8-13). A lunging thrust to the stomach is made by the attacker along the No. 5 angle of attack (Step 1). The defender moves his body off the line of attack and deflects the attacking arm by parrying with his left hand (Step 2). He deflects the attacking hand toward his right side by redirecting it with his right hand. As he does this, the defender can strike downward with the left forearm or the wrist onto the forearm or wrist of the attacker (Step 3). The defender ends up in a position to lock the elbow of the attacking arm across his body if he steps off the line of attack properly (Step 4).

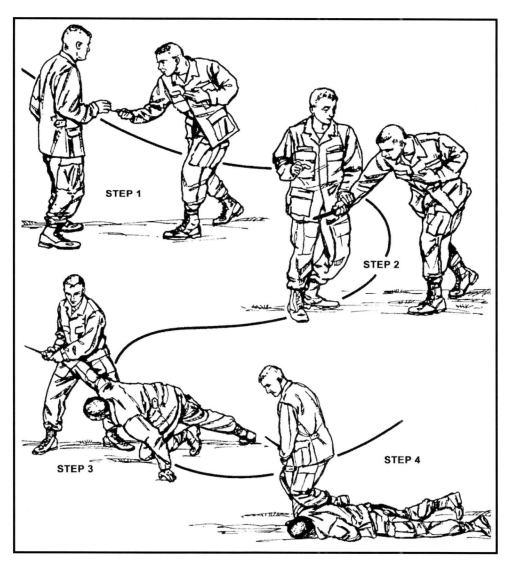

Figure 8-13. Low No. 5 angle of defense—parry.

(6) ***High No. 5 Angle of Defense*** (Figure 8-14). The attacker lunges with a thrust to the face, throat, or solar plexus (Step 1). The defender moves his body off the line of attack while parrying with either hand. He redirects the attacking arm so that the knife clears his body (Step 2). He maintains control of the weapon hand or arm and gouges the eyes of the attacker, driving him backward and off balance (Step 3). If the attacker is much taller than the defender, it may be a more natural movement for the defender to raise his left hand to strike and deflect the attacking arm. He can then gouge his thumb or fingers into the jugular notch of the attacker and force him to the ground. Still another possibility for a high No. 5 angle of attack is for the defender to move his body off the line of attack while parrying. He can then turn his body, rotate his shoulder under the elbow joint of the attacker, and lock it out (Step 4).

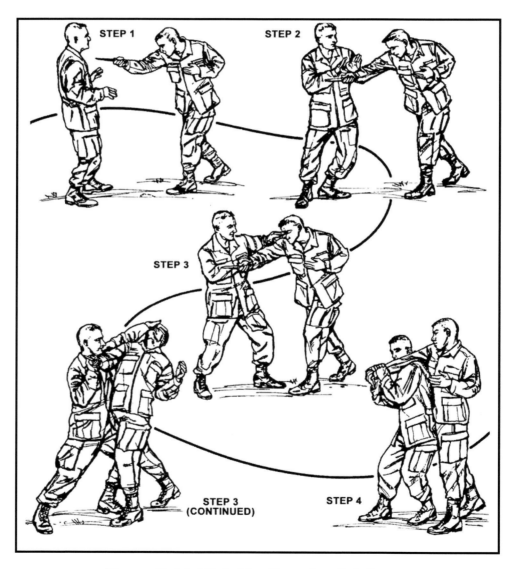

Figure 8-14. High No. 5 angle of defense.

(7) *No. 6 Angle of Defense* (Figure 8-15). The attacker strikes straight downward onto the defender with a stab (Step 1). The defender reacts by moving his body out of the weapon's path and by parrying or checking and redirecting the attacking arm, as the movement in the high No. 5 angle of defense (Step 2). The reactions may vary as to what is natural for the defender. The defender then takes control of the weapon and disarms the attacker (Step 3).

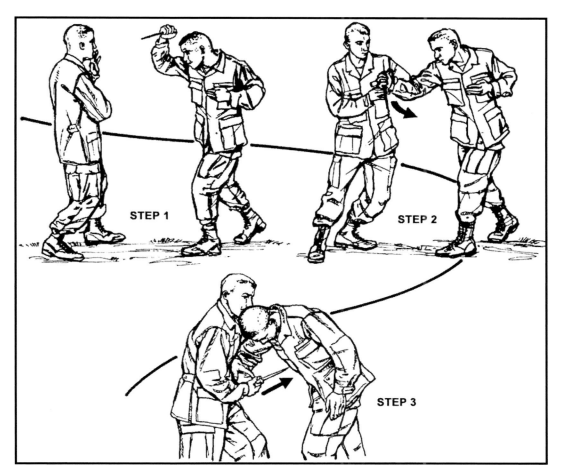

Figure 8-15. No. 6 angle of defense.

c. **Follow-Up Techniques**. Once the instructor believes the soldiers are skilled in these basic reactions to attack, follow-up techniques may be introduced and practiced. These drills make up the defense possibilities against the various angles of attack. They also enable the soldier to apply the principles of defense against weapons and allow him to feel the movements. Through repetition, the reactions become natural, and the soldier instinctively reacts to a knife attack with the proper defense. It is important not to associate specific movements or techniques with certain types of attack. The knife fighter must rely on his knowledge of principles and his training experience in reacting to a knife attack. No two attacks or reactions will be the same; thus, memorizing techniques will not ensure a soldier's survival.

(1) **Defend and Clear**. When the defender has performed a defensive maneuver and avoided an attack, he can push the attacker away and move out of the attacker's reach.

(2) **Defend and Stun**. After the defender performs his first defensive maneuver to a safer position, he can deliver a stunning blow as an immediate counterattack. Strikes to motor nerve points or attacker's limbs, low kicks, and elbow strikes are especially effective stunning techniques.

(3) **Defend and Disarm**. The defender also follows up his first defensive maneuver by maintaining control of the attacker's weapon arm, executing a stunning technique, and disarming the attacker. The stun distracts the attacker and also gives the defender some time to gain possession of the weapon and to execute his disarming technique.

8-5. UNARMED DEFENSE AGAINST A RIFLE WITH FIXED BAYONET

Defense against a rifle with a fixed bayonet involves the same principles as knife defense. The soldier considers the same angles of attack and the proper response for any attack along each angle.

a. Regardless of the type weapon used by the enemy, his attack will always be along one of the nine angles of attack at any one time. The soldier must get his entire body off the line of attack by moving to a safe position. A rifle with a fixed bayonet has two weapons: a knife at one end and a butt stock at the other end. The soldier will be safe as long as he is not in a position where he can be struck by either end during the attack.

b. Usually, he is in a more advantageous position if he moves inside the length of the weapon. He can then counterattack to gain control of the situation as soon as possible. The following counterattacks can be used as defenses against a rifle with a fixed bayonet; they also provide a good basis for training.

(1) **Unarmed Defense Against No. 1 Angle of Attack** (Figure 8-16). The attacker prepares to slash along the No. 1 angle of attack (Step 1). The defender waits until the last possible moment before moving so he is certain of the angle along which the attack is directed (Step 2). This way, the attacker cannot change his attack in response to movement by the defender. When the defender is certain that the attack is committed along a specific angle (No. 1, in this case), he moves to the inside of the attacker and gouges his eyes (Step 2) while the other hand redirects and controls the weapon. He maintains control of the weapon and lunges his entire body weight into the eye gouge to drive the attacker backward and off balance. The defender now ends up with the weapon, and the attacker is in a poor recovery position (Step 3).

Figure 8-16. Unarmed defense against No. 1 angle of attack.

(2) *Unarmed Defense Against No. 2 Angle of Attack* (Figure 8-17). The attacker makes a diagonal slash along the No. 2 angle of attack (Step 1). Again, the defender waits until he is sure of the attack before moving. The defender then moves to the outside of the attacker and counterattacks with a thumb jab into the right armpit (Step 2). He receives the momentum of the attacking weapon and controls it with his free hand. He uses the attacker's momentum against him by pulling the weapon in the direction it is going with one hand and pushing with his thumb of the other hand (Step 3). The attacker is completely off balance, and the defender can gain control of the weapon.

Figure 8-17. Unarmed defense against No. 2 angle of attack.

(3) *Unarmed Defense Against No. 3 Angle of Attack* (Figure 8-18). The attacker directs a horizontal slash along the No. 3 angle of attack (Step 1). The defender turns and moves to the inside of the attacker; he then strikes with his thumb into the jugular notch (Step 2). His entire body mass is behind the thumb strike and, coupled with the incoming momentum of the attacker, the strike drives the attacker's head backward and takes his balance (Step 3). The defender turns his body with the momentum of the weapon's attack to strip the weapon from the attacker's grip (Step 4).

Figure 8-18. Unarmed defense against No. 3 angle of attack.

(4) *Unarmed Defense Against No. 4 Angle of Attack* (Figure 8-19). The attack is a horizontal slash along the No. 4 angle of attack (Step 1). The defender moves in to the outside of the attacker (Step 2). He then turns with the attack, delivering an elbow strike to the throat (Step 3). At the same time, the defender's free hand controls the weapon and pulls it from the attacker as he is knocked off balance from the elbow strike.

Figure 8-19. Unarmed defense against No. 4 angle of attack.

(5) *Unarmed Defense Against Low No. 5 Angle of Attack*. (Figure 8-20). The attacker thrusts the bayonet at the stomach of the defender (Step 1). The defender shifts his body to the side to avoid the attack and to gouge the eyes of the attacker (Step 2). The defender's free hand maintains control of and strips the weapon from the attacker as he is driven backward with the eye gouge (Step 3).

Figure 8-20. Unarmed defense against low No. 5 angle of attack.

(6) *Unarmed Defense Against High No. 5 Angle of Attack* (Figure 8-21). The attacker delivers a thrust to the throat of the defender (Step 1). The defender then shifts to the side to avoid the attack, parries the thrust, and controls the weapon with his trail hand (Step 2). He then shifts his entire body mass forward over the lead foot, slamming a forearm strike into the attacker's throat (Step 3).

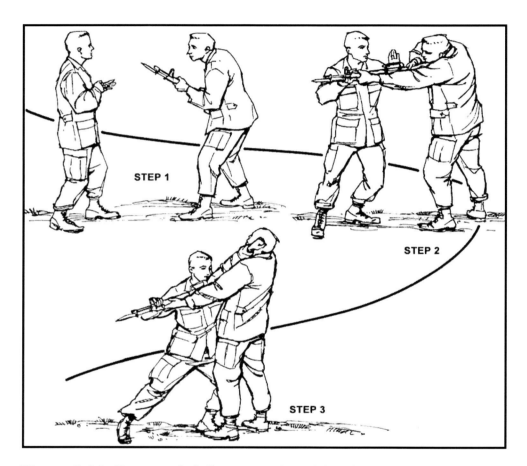

Figure 8-21. Unarmed defense against high No. 5 angle of attack.

(7) *Unarmed Defense Against No. 6 Angle of Attack* (Figure 8-22). The attacker delivers a downward stroke along the No. 6 angle of attack. The defender shifts to the outside to get off the line of attack and he grabs the weapon (Step 1). Then, he pulls the attacker off balance by causing him to overextend himself (Step 2). The defender shifts his weight backward and causes the attacker to fall, as he strips the weapon from him (Step 3).

Figure 8-22. Unarmed defense against No. 6 angle of attack.

CHAPTER 9
GROUP TACTICS

Most hand-to-hand situations on the battlefield will involve several people. Varying levels of force will be appropriate based on the situation and rules of engagement. Whether there are more friendlies or enemies, or whether or not some of the parties are armed, soldiers should enter a fight with a well-rehearsed plan and an overall fight strategy.

Section I. LETHAL FORCE SCENARIOS

The fundamental truth of hand-to-hand fighting is that the winner will be the one whose buddies show up first with a weapon. Given modern equipment, complicated scenarios, and the split seconds available to make life and death decisions, soldiers must be armed with practical and workable solutions.

9-1. RANGE

You will usually find yourself in a hand-to-hand situation unexpectedly; for example, your weapon jams when entering a room during MOUT. The first thing you must do is determine the appropriate actions to take, which will primarily be based on the range to the enemy. Against an armed enemy, the deciding factor of range is whether or not you can close the gap before the enemy can bring his weapon to bear.

   a. **Close Range.** If you are near enough to the enemy to close before he can bring his weapon to bear, you should immediately close the distance and gain control of him.

   b. **Long Range.** If the range is too great, or the enemy has sufficient time to bring his weapon to bear, the only options are to escape or take cover. Give your buddy a clear shot or get where you can clear your weapon to get yourself back in the fight.

9-2. CONTROL

If you have closed the distance, your primary goal is to control the enemy. This means controlling his ability to influence the rest of the fight, and controlling his ability to damage you. You are essentially stalling until someone can come to your aid.

   a. **Body Control.** You must control the enemy's ability to move, which can done by gaining and maintaining a dominant body position. This can also be accomplished by pinning the enemy in place (for example, against the wall).

   b. **Weapon Control.** You must immobilize the enemy's weapon. For example, use your weight to pin his rifle to his chest while you are mounted, or keep him from drawing a side arm by controlling it in the holster. You must also keep your weapons away from the enemy. It does you no good to immobilize the enemy if he can reach your side arm.

9-3. FINISHING

A very conservative approach should be taken to finishing moves. You must remember that the primary means of winning the fight is with the aid of your buddy. Any move that, if unsuccessful, would compromise your ability to control the situation should not be attempted.

Section II. RESTRICTIVE FORCE SCENARIOS

The most common error when fighting in groups is to enter the fight without a plan. This results in uncoordinated actions, and often in working against each other. Only practice gives soldiers the necessary confidence in themselves and their comrades and the ability to think and act together under the stress of hand-to-hand combat.

9-4. TWO AGAINST ONE

When fighting two against one, use the following procedures.

a. **Angles of Attack.** The fighters should advance together, spreading out so that if the enemy turns to face either soldier he will expose his flank to the other.

b. **Communication.** One soldier should attack the enemy's legs and the other should concentrate on his upper body. This can be done by signal, or the soldier attacking the flank can automatically go low. After the enemy is on the ground, good communication is necessary so that you can control and then finish him.

9-5. THREE AGAINST TWO

When fighting three against two, use the following procedures.

a. **Angles of Attack.** The fighters should advance so that the outside two are outside of the enemy. One of the enemies will have to make a choice to face either the outside or inside man. When he does, he will expose his flank to the other one. The fighter who is facing his opponent alone will stall until the other two have finished and can come to his aid.

b. **Communication.** Not only must the two who are fighting the same opponent communicate with each other, but also the fighter who is alone must keep them abreast of his situation. If he is in trouble, it may be necessary for one of them to disengage and come to his aid.

9-6. PARITY

If both groups have the same number of fighters, one fighter stays in reserve until the enemy has committed their entire force. When they have committed, the reserved fighter will attack the exposed back of the enemy.

9-7. ONE AGAINST TWO

When fighting one against two, use the following procedures.

a. **Remain Standing.** Defeating two opponents simultaneously is very difficult. When outnumbered, you should usually try to remain standing—mobility is critical to an effective defense or escape. It is very important not to expose your back. You must use the obstacles around you to restrict the enemies' movements so that you face only one at a time, or maneuver yourself to the flank of the one nearest to you and use him to block the other one. Attack the first enemy using strikes or field-expedient weapons, and then deal with the remaining one.

b. **Defense on the Ground.** If you should lose your footing or be taken to the ground, you must protect your back. Your best defense is to move into a corner or against a wall. Use a modified guard, so that your legs are not exposed, to limit the enemies' ability to attack simultaneously.

9-8.   TWO AGAINST THREE

When fighting two against three, you should maneuver to the flanks either together or separately.

a. **Together.** If you can get to one flank together, with the help of restrictive terrain if possible, use strikes to attack one opponent at a time until you have defeated all three.

b. **Separately.** If you are separated, one of you defends as in one against two while the other attacks the remaining enemy with strikes and then comes to the aid of the first.

APPENDIX A
SITUATIONAL TRAINING

A successful combatives program cannot stand alone. The transition to the appropriate techniques must be natural, which can only be accomplished by integrating combatives into scenario training. This is hard and arduous training; soldiers should know that war is harsh, and the reality of training for war is equally harsh.

Section I. PLANNING CONSIDERATIONS

Training soldiers in the appropriate use of combatives requires expertise and detailed planning. As in live-fire training, the potential for accidents must be mitigated by control of both the scenario and the conduct of the exercise itself.

A-1. PLANNING

When planning a hand-to-hand scenario many factors must be addressed. A detailed and well thought out scenario tells the soldiers what type of techniques are appropriate. For example, very different techniques are appropriate when clearing a building in an enemy occupied city, such as when U.S. forces cleared Hue City, Vietnam, than when clearing a building during a noncombatant evacuation operation.

a. **Scenario.** Scenarios must be explained to soldiers in detail so that the appropriate actions come to them naturally. This should include an explanation of the events leading up to the scenario as well as the immediate tactical situation.

b. **Rules of Engagement**. Rules of engagement must be given that provide soldiers a clear understanding of what actions are appropriate.

A-2. CONDUCT

During the conduct of an exercise, leaders must maintain control throughout. It is very easy for undisciplined troops to go beyond the bounds of the exercise when they get frustrated at their own poor training. Soldiers and subordinate leaders must know what is expected of them, and what the repercussions are for inappropriate actions.

a. **Opposing Force.** There is always a tendency for soldiers playing the opposing force (OPFOR) to lose track of the training goals and get carried away. OPFOR must be well rehearsed and stay within the bounds of the scenario. The safety of the OPFOR must be considered even in small details of the situation. For example:

- Should they wear their canteens on their LBE knowing they will be knocked down?
- Are there any dangerous objects for them to fall on, such as the pointed corner of a table or a picket in the ground?

b. **Safety Measures.** The most important control measure that a leader can have after the scenario begins is a means to stop the action. This can be as simple as a whistle, but it must be clear and easily heard over the action.

Section II. EXAMPLE SCENARIOS

There are as many different possible scenarios as there are potential missions. Commanders must evaluate their own METL to come up with realistic scenarios for their units. One of the primary learning objectives is the thought that must go into using techniques and tactics that are appropriate to the situation.

A-3. ROOM CLEARING

Clearing buildings during MOUT can confront soldiers at the lowest level with life and death decisions at every turn.

a. **Situation.** The battalion has been deployed to the island nation of Cortina to help stabilize the political situation long enough for the recently elected democratic government to gain control of the country. Platoons are being sent out to search for suspected weapons cached by the former armed forces, who recently lost power. Your platoon has been tasked to search and clear a small village.

b. **Rules of Engagement.** Deadly force is only authorized for self-defense, defense of others, or defense of property that could create a substantial risk to others.

A-4. TRENCH CLEARING

Soldiers must always be trained and ready to execute their principal wartime missions.

a. **Situation.** The platoon is attacking an enemy-held bunker complex.

b. **Rules of Engagement.** Deadly force is authorized in keeping with the law of war.

A-5. ROADBLOCK

Soldiers may be used in increasingly more complex scenarios short of war.

a. **Situation.** The platoon is manning roadblocks that divide the two hostile factions of Cortina. Hostile crowds are known to appear, threatening U.S. soldiers.

b. **Rules of Engagement.** Soldiers will use the minimum amount of force necessary to control the situation.

APPENDIX B
COMPETITIONS

A look at the history of combatives systems reveals two fundamental mistakes, both of which are related to competition. The first mistake is having no form of competition, which is generally due to the thought that the techniques are "too dangerous" for competitions. Although many techniques are too dangerous for live competition, many benefits can be gained by competing even in a limited set of techniques. The boxer is a better puncher than the traditional martial artist not because of the mechanics of punching, but because his technique has been refined through competition.

Competitions are useful for military units for many other reasons. The problem of developing is really the problem of how to Competitions can motivate subordinate unit leaders to emphasize combatives training, which leads to a strong unit program. Competitions also encourage the pursuit of excellence in soldiers.

The other mistake is that once a method of competition has been selected, training will naturally become focused on winning at competition rather than on winning in combat. To gain the benefits from competition without falling into the trap of a competitive focus, the unit must have a graduated system of competition rules. In this way there will be no competitive advantage to training specifically for competitions. Those who do will find themselves unprepared for the additional techniques that are allowed at the next level of competition. This also allows for a very safe subset of techniques to be used at the lower levels without loosing the combat focus.

Three sets of rules govern combatives competition—basic, standard, and special. Although other combative sports are encouraged, they sometimes reinforce bad combative habits.

B-1. BASIC COMPETITIONS
The basic competition rules are designed for entry-level soldiers, or soldiers with a limited knowledge base. Soldiers will begin with a handshake, face each other on their knees, and fight until submission or for a designated time limit. On reaching the time limit, a winner will be designated by the referee based upon aggressiveness and display of superior technique.

B-2. STANDARD COMPETITIONS
Standard competitions are conducted using the following guidelines.

  a. **Uniform**. Soldiers compete wearing BDUs and PT shoes. For ease in scoring, one soldier may wear a DBDU top.

  b. **Duration**. Matches last six to ten minutes. Specific match duration is decided in advance.

c. **Scoring**. Points are awarded to establish good fight habits and emphasize the importance of dominant body position. Submission will end the fight regardless of the score. All positions must be stabilized to the judge's satisfaction to earn points. The point values are:

2 Points	Take Down: From the standing position, the fighter places his opponent on the ground but fails to gain dominant position.
3 Points	Take Down: From the standing position, the fighter places his opponent on his back and gains side control or the mount.
3 Points	Pass the Guard: From between his opponent's legs, the fighter clears the legs and gains side control or the mount.
3 Points	Sweep: From the guard position, the fighter changes positions, placing his opponent on his back.
3 Points	Knee in Chest: From side control, the fighter establishes one knee in his opponent's chest and or abdomen and the other knee up and away from him and stabilizes himself.
4 Points	Mount: The fighter establishes the mount with both knees and feet on the ground.
4 Points	Back Mount: The fighter establishes the back mount with both feet hooked in position.
1 Point deduction:	Stalling: From either within the guard or side control, the fighter must try to improve his position. The judge will give two warnings and then subtract a point. If the stalling continues, the judge gives two additional warnings, then subtracts an additional point, continuing this pattern until the end of the match or action is conducted.

d. **Judging**. Each match has one judge and one score keeper. It is the judge's responsibility to ensure a safe and fair match. All decisions are final.

e. **Illegal Techniques**. The following are illegal and dangerous techniques. Their use may result in disqualification:

- Strikes of any kind.
- Twisting knee locks.
- Finger techniques.
- Wrist techniques.
- Grabbing the fingers.
- Toe holds.
- Attacking the groin.
- Picking up the opponent to pass the guard.

f. **Tie Breaking**. If the score is tied at the end of the allotted time, the match will continue until the next point is scored or deducted.

g. **Time Limits**. Although time limits tend to change the types of techniques commonly employed, they are necessary, especially when conducting a large number of matches (as in a tournament). If time limits are used, a specific time limit will be decided on in advance, commensurate with the number of matches to be conducted. An alternative to time limits is to have a set amount of maximum points (usually fifteen). The first fighter to reach that limit is the winner. A victory by submission is far preferable to a point victory.

B-3.   SPECIAL COMPETITION
Special competitions are conducted using the following guidelines.
  a. **Required Safety Gear and Uniform Safety Gear.**
    • Approved shin and instep pads (pull on type), approved knee pads, cup, mouth guard.
    • Optional—Neoprene or cloth ankle supports can be worn to support a previous injury but the injury must be verified by the ringside physician and the supports must be approved. Taping of previously injured areas will be under the same condition as stated above.
  b. **Uniform.**
  (1) Fighters will fight bare top, or with approved athletic top for females.
  (2) Full-length tights or bicycle-length tights will be worn on the lower half of the body.
  (3) Kneepads are required and must be of approved thickness and density.
  (4) Shin and instep (pull on type) pads must be approved for thickness and density as well as proper fit. They must provide maximum softness with enough density so that the shin and knee bones cannot be felt when strong pressure is applied. Pads must fit snugly so they will not easily pull down or move around during competition.
  (5) Fighters must wear a cup. If the fighter wears an outer cup it must cover only the groin and lower bladder area; it cannot extend out around the hip area. Outer cups must be approved.
  c. **Illegal Techniques.**
    • Head butts.
    • Closed fist strikes to the head.
    • Striking with the elbows.
    • Groin strikes.
    • Straight palm strikes to the face.
    • Kicks and knee strikes to a downed opponent.
    • Striking the throat.
    • Pulling hair.
    • Poking or gouging eyes.
    • Biting.
    • Throwing an opponent onto their head or neck.
    • Heel hooks.
    • Grabbing the ring ropes.
    • Pinching (intentional).
    • Scratching (intentional).
    • Striking the side and or front of the knee.
    • Knee strikes to the face.
    • Finger and toe submissions.
  d. **Additional Illegal Acts.** Fighters may not use any slippery substance on their body such as petroleum jelly or liniment.

   e. **Legal Techniques.**
- Slapping with the open hand palm side only.
- Kicking the legs, body, or head (when both fighters are standing).
- Punching the body.
- Takedowns with the exceptions noted above.
- Submission, joint locks, chokes, and pressure point techniques except as noted.
- Knee strikes to both the legs and body (while both fighters are standing).

   f. **Length of Matches.** Matches will be at least five minutes. Longer matches may be coordinated.

   g. **Methods of Victory.**
- Win by knockout (KO).
- Win by technical knockout (TKO).
- Win by "tap out."
- Win by verbal submission.
- Win by choke out.
- Win by referee stoppage.
- Win by judges' decision.
- Win by disqualification.

   h. **Disqualification.**
- Use of any illegal joint technique will result in immediate disqualification.
- Intentional use of any illegal technique will result in immediate disqualification.
- Any unsportsman-like conduct may result in disqualification.

   i. **Definitions of Methods of Victory.** The methods of victory are defined as follows:

(1) ***Knockout (KO).*** If one fighter goes down from the impact of a blow (not from a push, slip, or throw), the referee will send the fighter who struck the blow to a neutral corner and begin a 10 count. If the downed fighter cannot return to his feet before 10 is reached, a knockout is awarded.

(2) ***Technical Knockout (TKO).*** A TKO is registered when the referee deems that one fighter cannot defend himself and is in danger of receiving excessive damage if the match continues. In this case, the referee will award the other fighter a TKO victory.

(3) ***"Tap Out."*** A fighter may give up at any time during the match by "tapping out." This is done by slapping their open palm several times (a minimum of twice) on the mat, The referee acknowledges a victory for the opponent and ends the match immediately.

(4) ***Verbal Submission.*** A fighter may give up at any time during the match by saying "stop" loud enough for the referee to hear. The referee will stop the fight and award the victory to the other fighter.

(5) ***Choke Out.*** When a choke has been applied, the referee will watch for any sign of unconsciousness, including failure to respond to verbal questions, and immediately stop the match, awarding the victory to the fighter who applied the choke.

(6) ***Referee Stoppage.*** The referee will consider both combatants' safety at all times. He may stop the match if he thinks that a fighter's safety is in danger and or an injury is eminent. This is especially important when a joint lock is being applied and the "locked"

fighter refuses to "tap out" or verbally submit. The referee will award the victory to the appropriate fighter.

(7) ***Judges' Decision.*** The match will be judged by three judges. When a match goes to the time limit, the judges will make a decision based on the following point system.

(a) *Standing Superiority.* The fighter who shows superior skills on his feet will be awarded one point and the opponent no points. In the case of equal display of standing skills, both fighters will be awarded one point.

(b) *Takedown Superiority.* The fighter who shows superiority in takedowns will be awarded one point and the opponent no points. In the case of equal display of takedown skills, both fighters will be awarded one point.

(c) *Ground Superiority.* The fighter who shows superiority in ground fighting will be awarded one point and the opponent no points. In the case that neither fighter displays superiority during ground fighting, both fighters will be awarded one point.

(d) *Total Superiority.* The fighter who controls most of the action during the match will be awarded two points. In the case that neither fighter controls most of the action, both fighters will be awarded no points.

The points will be totaled and the fighter with the most points will be judged as the winner by each individual judge. The judges will turn in their scorecard with their name on it at the end of the match. The referee will award a decision based on the decision of the judges as follows:

- Unanimous decision. All three judges awarded victory to the same fighter.
- Majority decision. Two judges award a victory to the same fighter and the third judge scores the fight a draw, or one judge awards a victory to one fighter and the other two score the fight a draw.
- Split decision. Two judges award a decision to the same fighter and the third judge awards a decision to the other fighter.
- Draw. All three judges score the match a draw or one judge scores the fight a draw and the other two judges are split.

j.   **Stalemate.** When the combatants are on the ground and neither is attempting to gain an advantage position or submission, the referee will start a 30-second count. If neither fighter attempts to improve his position or gain a submission, a stalemate exists and the referee will break the fighters and restart them on their feet. When the fighters go under the ropes or become entangled with the ropes the referee calls "STOP" and drags them into the center of the ring. The referee will ensure that neither fighter gains advantage from this movement before restarting with the command "FIGHT."

k. **Weigh-In Procedures and Weight Classes.** Fighters may weigh in the evening before or up to one hour before the fight. No fighter should weigh in more than 24 hours before the fight. Fighters will be paired by weight class. Sponsoring units may create their own weight classes. Suggested weight classes are as follows:

Super Heavyweight	Over 220 pounds
Heavyweight	220 and under
Super Light Heavyweight	205 and under
Light Heavyweight	195 and under
Cruiser Weight	185 and under
Super Middleweight	175 and under
Middleweight	165 and under
Light Middleweight	155 and under
Super Welterweight	145 and under
Welterweight	135 and under
Super Lightweight	125 and under
Lightweight	115 and under
Bantamweight	105 and under

GLOSSARY

AIT	advanced infantry training
BDU	basic duty uniform
DBDU	desert basic duty uniform
FSN	Federal stock number
IAW	in accordance with
KO	knockout
LBE	load-bearing equipment
LCE	load-carrying equipment
METL	mission-essential task list
MOUT	military operations on urban terrain
OPFOR	opposing force
OSUT	one-station unit training
PT	physical training
TKO	technical knockout
TSC	Training Support Center
U.S.	United States

REFERENCES

DOCUMENTS NEEDED

These documents must be available to the intended users of this publication.

*FM 21-20   Physical Fitness Training. 30 September 1992.

---

*This source was also used to develop this publication.

INDEX

attacks, 4-1
  double leg attack, 5-24 (illus, 5-24, 5-25)
    finishes from, 5-25
      hook the leg, 5-27 (illus)
      lift, 5-25 (illus, 5-25 thru 5-27)
  from the guard, 4-30
    arm lock, 4-30 (illus, 4-30, 4-31)
    guillotine choke, 4-32 (illus, 4-32, 4-33)
    sweeps, 4-34
      ankle grab/knee push, 4-37 (illus 4-37 thru 4-39)
      Captain Kirk, 4-36 (illus)
      scissors, 4-34 (illus, 4-34, 4-35)
    triangle choke, 4-39 (illus 4-39, 4-40)
  from the back mount, 4-25
    collar choke, 4-25 (illus, 4-25, 4-26)
    single wing choke, 4-27 (illus, 4-27, 4-28)
    straight arm bar, 4-28 (illus, 4-28, 4-29)
  from the mount, 4-14
    leaning choke, 4-16 (illus, 4-16, 4-17)
    nutcracker choke, 4-17 (illus, 4-17, 4-18)
    paper cutter choke, 4-15 (illus, 4-15, 4-16)
    sleeve choke, 4-18 (illus, 4-18, 4-19)
  from the rear, 5-31 (illus)
  knee mount, 4-41 (illus, 4-41, 4-42)
    chokes, 4-45 (illus, 4-45, 4-46)
    straight arm bar, 4-47 (illus 4-47, 4-48)
      variation, 4-51 (illus)
  leg attack, 4-52
    figure-four ankle lock, 4-54 (illus)
    straight ankle lock, 4-52 (illus, 4-52 thru 4-54)
    straight knee bar, 4-55 (illus, 4-55, 4-56)
  pass the guard, 4-2
    closed guard, 4-2 (illus, 4-3 thru 4-11)
    open guard, 4-11 (illus, 4-11 thru 4-14)
  single leg attacks, 5-28 (illus)
    block opposite knee, 5-30 (illus)
    dump, 5-29 (illus)
    leg sweep, 5-30 (illus)
  triple attack, 4-20
    gain the back mount, 4-24 (illus)
    lapel choke, 4-20 (illus, 4-20, 4-21)
    straight arm bar, 4-22 (illus, 4-22, 4-23)

bayonet assault course, 2-6
  layout, 2-6 (illus, 2-7)
  obstacles, 2-8 (illus, 2-9 thru 2-12)
  safety, 2-6
  standards, 2-12
  targets, 2-7 (illus, 2-8)
  usage, 2-8
body positioning moves, 3-4
  arm push and roll to the rear mount, 3-18 (illus, 3-18 thru 3-21)
  escape the half guard, 3-16 (illus, 3-16, 3-17)
  escape the mount, shrimp to the guard, 3-8 (illus, 3-9 thru 3-11)
  escape the mount, trap, and roll, 3-6 (illus, 3-7, 3-8)
  escape the rear mount, 3-21 (illus, 3-21 thru 3-23)

pass the guard and achieve the mount, 3-11 (illus, 3-11 thru 3-15)
stand up in base, 3-1 (illus, 3-5, 3-6)
body positions
  advanced, 4-1
    knee in the stomach, 4-2 (illus)
    north-south position, 4-1 (illus)
  dominant, 3-1
    back mount, 3-1 (illus, 3-2)
    front mount, 3-2 (illus, 3-3)
    guard, 3-3 (illus)
    side control, 3-4 (illus)
breakfall, 5-1
  forward rolling, 5-3 (illus)
  forward rolling from the kneeling position, 5-1 (illus, 5-2, 5-3)
  rear, 5-4 (illus)
  side position, 5-1 (illus)

chokes
  collar, 4-22 (illus, 4-25, 4-26)
  cross collar, 3-26 (illus, 3-26 thru 3-28)
  front guillotine, 3-29 (illus, 3-29 thru 3-31)
  from knee mount, 4-45 (illus, 4-45, 4-46)
  guillotine, 4-32 (illus, 4-32, 4-33)
    defend, 5-13 (illus, 5-13 thru 5-15)
      with knee strikes, 5-15 (illus, 5-15, 5-16)
  lapel, 4-20 (illus, 4-20, 4-21)
  leaning, 4-16 (illus, 4-16, 4-17)
  nutcracker, 4-17 (illus, 4-17, 4-18)
  paper cutter, 4-15 (illus, 4-15, 4-16)
  rear naked, 3-24 (illus, 3-24, 3-25)
  single wing, 4-27 (illus, 4-27, 4-28)
  sleeve, 4-18 (illus, 4-18, 4-19)
  triangle, 4-39 (illus, 4-39, 4-40)
clinch, 5-4
  close range, 5-4 (illus, 5-5, 5-6)
  long range, 5-6
combatives
  formations, 2-4
    matted rooms, 2-5

sawdust pit, 2-5
    construction, 2-5 (illus)
principles, 1-1, 1-2
safety, 1-2
  bayonet assault course, 2-6
  chokes, 1-2
  general, 1-2
  joint locks, 1-2
  supervision, 1-2
  striking, 1-2
  training areas, 1-2
trainers, 2-1
  responsibilities, 2-1
training, 1-1, 2-1
  basic, 2-3
  effects, 1-1
  one-station unit, 2-3
  purpose, 1-1
  sustainment, 2-4
competitions, B-1
  basic, B-1
  standard, B-1
    duration, B-1
    illegal techniques, B-2
    judging, B-2
    scoring, B-2
    tie-breaking, B-2
    time limits, B-2
    uniform, B-1
  special, B-3
    disqualification, B-4
    illegal techniques, B-3
    legal techniques, B-4
    length, B-4
    methods of victory, B-4
      definitions, B-4, B-5
    safety gear, B-3
    stalemate, B-5
    uniform, B-3
    weigh-in, B-6

finishing moves, 3-24
  bent arm bar from the mount, 3-31 (illus, 3-31 thru 3-33)
  cross collar choke, 3-26 (illus, 3-26 thru 3-28)

front guillotine choke, 3-29 (illus, 3-29 thru 3-31)

rear naked choke, 3-24 (illus, 3-24, 3-25)

straight arm bar from the guard, 3-35 (illus, 3-35 thru 3-38)

straight arm bar from the mount, 3-33 (illus, 3-33 thru 3-35)

sweep from attempted straight arm bar, 3-39 (illus, 3-39, 3-40)

ground-fighting techniques
basic, 3-1
advanced, 4-1

handheld weapons, 7-1
angles of attack, 7-1 (illus 7-1 thru 7-6)
bayonet/knife, 7-22
knife-against-knife sequence, straight grip, 7-22
knife fighter's stance, 7-23 (illus)
modified stance, 7-24 (illus)
range, 7-24
reverse grip, 7-23, 7-25 (illus, 7-25 thru 7-28)
development, 7-6
field-expedient, 7-29
entrenching tool, 7-29 (illus, 7-29 thru 7-32)
six-foot pole, 7-36 (illus)
three-foot stick, 7-33 (illus, 7-34, 7-35)
fighting techniques, 7-6
fixed bayonet, 7-2
movements, 7-8
attack, 7-9
butt stroke, 7-11 (illus, 7-12)
slash, 7-13 (illus)
smash, 7-14 (illus)
thrust, 7-10 (illus, 7-11)
crossover, 7-9 (illus)
defensive, 7-15
block, 7-17 (illus, 7-18 thru 7-22)
parry, 7-15 (illus, 7-15, 7-16)

modified, 7-21 (illus)
whirl, 7-9 (illus)
follow-up, 7-22
position, 7-7
attack, 7-7 (illus)
relaxed, 7-8 (illus)
principles, 7-7
hand-to-hand combat, iv
definition, 1-1
headlocks, 3-41, 5-13
defense against, 3-41 (illus, 3-41 thru 3-47), 5-13
with punches, 5-17 (illus, 5-17 thru 5-19)
without punches, 5-19 (illus, 5-19 thru 5-20)

scenarios, 9-1
examples, A-2
lethal force, 9-1
control, 9-1
finishing, 9-1
range, 9-1
restrictive force, 9-2
situational training, A-1
conduct, A-1
planning, A-1
standing defense, 8-1
against bear hugs, 8-7 thru 8-13 (illus, 8-7 thru 8-13)
against chokes, 8-1
standing rear naked, 8-1 (illus, 8-1 thru 8-2)
standing rear naked pulling back, 8-3 (illus, 8-3, 8-4)
against one-hand neck press, 8-5 (illus)
against two-hand neck press, 8-6 (illus, 8-6, 8-7)
strikes, 4-57
arm, 6-1
hook, 6-2 (illus, 6-3)
jab, 6-1 (illus)
reverse punch, 6-2 (illus)

uppercut, 6-3
>lead hand, 6-3 (illus, 6-3, 6-4)
>trail hand, 6-4 (illus, 6-4, 6-5)
>defending against, 4-65 (illus, 4-65 thru 4-67)
elbow, 6-5
>horizontal, 6-5 (illus)
>upward, 6-6 (illus)
from side control, 4-63 (illus, 4-63 thru 4-65)
kicks, 6-6
>lead leg front, 6-7 (illus)
>rear leg front, 6-7 (illus)
>shin, 6-8 (illus)
>stepping side, 6-8 (illus)
knee, 6-9 (illus)
pass the guard with, 4-57 (illus, 4-57 thru 4-62)
punching combinations, 6-6

takedowns, 5-1
basic, 5-7 (illus, 5-7, 5-8)
from against a wall, 5-21
>leg drag, 5-23 (illus, 5-23, 5-24)
>position and strikes, 5-21 (illus, 5-21 thru 5-23)
hip throw, 5-9 (illus, 5-9, 5-10)
hook the leg, 5-8 (illus)
rear, 5-10 (illus, 5-10 thru 5-12)
teaching techniques, 2-12
crawl, walk, run, 2-18
>first level, 2-18
>second level, 2-18
demonstrations, 2-18
>company-size formation or larger, 2-18
>platoon-size formation or smaller, 2-18
drills, 2-19, 3-40
execution, 2-19
>at combat speed, 2-19
>by-the-numbers, 2-19
protective equipment, 2-19
>other, 2-19
>pads, 2-19 (illus, 2-20)

stretches, 2-12, 2-13
back-roll stretch, 2-13 (illus)
buddy-assisted back stretch, 2-17 (illus)
buddy-assisted groin (butterfly) stretch, 2-16 (illus)
buddy-assisted hamstring stretch, 2-15 (illus)
buddy-assisted splits, 2-14 (illus)
warm-ups, 2-12, 2-13

unarmed defense, 8-13
against a knife, 8-14 thru 8-21 (illus, 8-15 thru 8-21)
against a rifle with fixed bayonet, 8-22 thru 8-29 (illus, 8-23 thru 8-29)
against an armed opponent, 8-13